Little Girl Lost

Barbie Probert-Wright was a winner of the Richard & Judy competition TRUE. The series was executive produced by Simon and Amanda Ross, and produced by Gareth Jones and Zoe Russell-Stretten.

Little Girl Lost

BARBIE PROBERT-WRIGHT

with Jean Ritchie

arrow books

Published by Arrow Books in 2006

14 16 18 20 19 17 15 13

Copyright © Barbie Probert-Wright, 2006

Barbie Probert-Wright has asserted her right under the Copyright, Designs and Patents Act, 1988 to be identified as the author of this work.

Grateful acknowledgement is made to Dr Eva Brües for permission to reproduce 'Köln. Allerseelen 1944' by Otto Brües, and to Morag Perrott for her design of the map on p. xv.

The author and publishers have made all reasonable efforts to contact copyright holders for permission, and apologise for any omissions or errors in the form of credit given. Corrections may be made in future printings.

This book is a work of non-fiction based on the experiences and recollections of Barbie Probert-Wright. The author has warranted to the publishers that, except in such minor respects not affecting the substantial accuracy of the work, the contents of this book are true. Whilst the publishers have taken care to explore and check where reasonably possible, they have not verified all the information in this book and do not warrant its veracity in all respects.

First published in Great Britain in 2006 by
Arrow Books
Random House, 20 Vauxhall Bridge Road,
London SW1V 2SA

www.rbooks.co.uk

Addresses for companies within The Random House Group Limited can be found at:
www.randomhouse.co.uk/offices.htm

The Random House Group Limited Reg. No. 954009

A CIP catalogue record for this book
is available from the British Library

ISBN 9780099498490

The Random House Group Limited supports The Forest Stewardship Council (FSC), the leading international forest certification organisation. All our titles that are printed on Greenpeace approved FSC certified paper carry the FSC logo. Our paper procurement policy can be found at
www.rbooks.co.uk/environment.

Typeset in Spectrum MT by Palimpsest Book Production Limited, Polmont, Stirlingshire

Printed and bound in Great Britain by CPI Bookmarque, Croydon, CR0 4TD

This book is dedicated to the loving memory of my sister Eva, whose courage and determination got us through this journey alive, and to my husband Ray and my daughter Babette, with my fondest love.

I would also like to dedicate it to all children across the world whose lives today are being torn apart by the brutality of war.

Contents

Foreword

In the spring of 1945, in a dark and dangerous world of conflict and defeat, my sister saved my life.

The Second World War ripped apart the lives of millions of people and nobody who lived through it remained completely untouched by it. As a small child growing up in Germany, I was protected by my loving family from the horrific events that were ravaging Europe, and I remained innocent of the true nature of war until the final few months, when I was seven years old and we were on the brink of defeat and invasion. Then, no amount of love could protect me.

With my nineteen-year-old sister Eva, I was thrust into the maelstrom. Separated from our beloved mother, and with our father missing in action, we set out together to trek across Germany to find her, walking through battlefields, witnessing death first hand, sheltering from gunfire, sleeping rough and starving. I saw sights that no child should ever have to witness. I also met with incredible generosity and overwhelming kindness. I came to understand that enemies are united by their common humanity. I began to realise what sacrifice was and what really matters when you are faced with losing every single thing you own.

Into a few short months I packed a lifetime's experiences, observing them through the prism of my own childish innocence. It is only years later that I have come to understand fully what was going on around me and what happened to the two of us. It is only now that I fully appreciate the courage and selflessness of my sister Eva.

I am writing this in the sitting room of my comfortable home, where I live with my husband. On the table beside me is a tattered exercise book, filled with the dreams and memories of a girl writing sixty years ago. It is falling apart now and faded in places: there are yellowing scraps of newspaper, brittle old photographs and pasted cards inside it.

This is the diary that Eva kept throughout those months, writing in it sporadically, whenever she got the chance. It is the spine of this book, giving a framework to all my memories of what was to come. Its pages, coming loose after more than sixty years, are filled with diary entries, poems and quotations. Its very survival is remarkable and it is, perhaps, my most treasured possession. I owe my survival to Eva and she has also provided me with the means of writing this book. The memories of a child are sometimes dreamlike, blurry and disordered. Her diary has helped me put them all in place. This book is based on what she wrote, as well my own memories, and the details I gathered from when Eva and I would reminisce about our journey over the many years that followed. It is not a history of the war – though I have included details of the situation as it affected us — it is simply the story of two sisters, desperate to get home and struggling to survive. It is Eva's story, and my story.

Eva is now dead. I am not sure, if she were still alive, whether she would have wanted the attention this book brings her: she remained self-effacing, gentle and wholly concerned for others throughout her life. I don't want to make her sound too good to be true — she was also very jolly, with a fine sense of humour, and she knew how to enjoy herself. But she would never have sought praise for what she did. To her it came naturally. She loved me, so she protected and cared for me. No child could ever have asked for more.

———————

As I get older and the rhythms of my own day-to-day life are slowing, I find myself thinking more and more about the great events of those few months and feel ever closer to those times.

At the table beside me as I write, my grand-daughter Amy-Lou is sitting quietly, colouring in the pictures in her drawing book. Her fair head is bent down as she earnestly concentrates on her task. In a minute she will raise her head, fix me with those imploring eyes and say, 'Can we go and feed the ducks? Can we? Please?'

She is seven years old, the same age that I was when the main events of this story happened to me. I cannot imagine her ever having to face the sort of hardships that I did. I would hate her world ever to become a place where things like that can happen.

And yet, there are plenty of places around the globe where children are suffering as much as and more than I did. It breaks my heart to think of little ones, like my granddaughter, being subjected to the terror and hunger that we endured.

Even so, I do not regret what I went through. Young as I was, it forged my character, made me determined to see things through. It also made me realise, in a way that perhaps we all take too much for granted today, the sheer power of love. We were sustained throughout our travels by our love for our mother, and I was protected and cherished by Eva's love for me.

My book is a testament to that love.

The Route Taken by Barbie & Eva
Through Germany in 1945

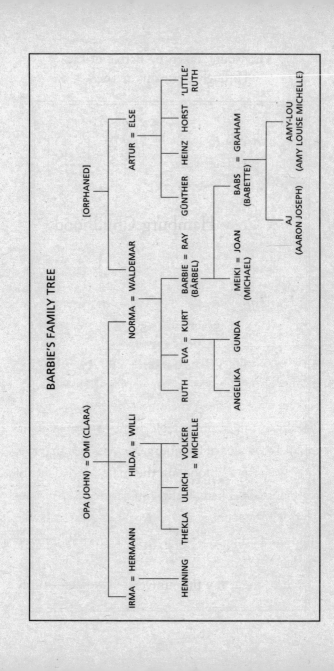

BARBIE'S FAMILY TREE

content, a world of innocence and happiness. Our life was nothing out of the ordinary. We lived, as thousands of Germans did, a normal, comfortable, domestic life. Soon this quiet, civilised world would be shattered for ever by the horrors of war but in the years before, as I grew from babyhood, everything was perfect. We lived in a spacious third-floor flat on the Wandsbecker Chaussee, a well-known main road in Hamburg, lined with impressive apartment blocks like ours. Our flat had a long, wide hallway in which there was room for me to have a swing, and to roller-skate up and down, and it had a balcony that overlooked the road below. One of my earliest memories is of sitting out on the balcony with a large bowl of gooseberries. I was four years old and had been given a blunt knife so I could top and tail them for my mother. The balcony immediately below our flat had an awning, and when I accidentally dropped a gooseberry over, it bounced down the taut fabric of the awning with a ping, ping, ping. What a wonderful noise! I thought and let another one fall over the side. Before long, I had dropped every single berry over the balcony, just to hear the sound they made.

When my mother saw this she was not pleased. 'Darling, what have you done? That's very naughty,' she scolded me. But even when she was trying to be cross with me, it was clear that she thought the whole incident rather funny. She said I would never again be trusted with a bowl of gooseberries on the balcony and from then on I had to sit inside to do them.

I was much younger than my two older sisters. Ruth was fourteen when I was born and Eva was twelve. It was like having three mothers, because they all fussed over me so much. I was not spoiled materially, and I was always required to be polite and well behaved. But the attention and love I received were wonderful, and the world of that apartment really did seem to revolve around me. My family always called me *Puppe*, which means little doll, or *Kleine*, little one. My full name is Bärbel, which is what I am still known as to my German family and friends, but when I came to live in England in 1957 people seemed to find it hard to say or remember and I became Barbie. As a tiny child, I was always on tiptoe, always dancing around the flat, always singing. I went to a kindergarten run by a motherly lady where we learned songs, invented our own make-believe games and did simple handicrafts. We were taken out in long 'crocodiles', all holding hands, to walk on the wide boulevard near the canal. We put on little plays and in one I was a snowflake, in another a rabbit. One Mother's Day I made a brightly coloured paper bouquet for my mother.

With my family I also went to a local sports club, where there were special facilities for small children and where I played with my best friend, a girl called Inge, who was a twin and was also in kindergarten with me.

By now the war was well under way, but I knew nothing of it. The dramas going on far away in other countries as German armies advanced across Europe did not impinge on my world. I was sheltered and protected by my adoring family. Whatever worries and fears they must have had about the great conflict and the changes taking place in our beloved country they kept well hidden. I knew nothing of them.

My father Waldemar – or Waldi, as my mother called him – was already forty when I was born and too old to be conscripted to fight in the war – at least at the beginning. He had fought in the First World War and had been shot down in a plane over the English Channel, permanently damaging one of his hands and sustaining other injuries. His age, war record, disabilities and the fact that he worked in a reserved occupation meant that he was able to stay at home with us. My father worked on the railways in a senior management job, detecting and preventing crime on the networks and trains.

Some time during the early years of the war he was sent to work in the Wartegau, or the Polish corridor. This was a zone of land which had been taken away from Germany at the end of the First World War and had been colonised by Poles. When Germany invaded Poland in 1939, most of these Poles were evacuated to southern Poland, and their farms and jobs were taken over by Germans. The Poles who had lived there before the first war by and large remained, but now worked for Germans, not for wealthy Poles. My father's job was to try to stamp out the smuggling that was rife there. Although he was working away, he was able to travel back to Hamburg regularly and was a familiar part of my early childhood.

The estate was vast and Uncle Hermann had to go round it every day to oversee the workers. He used a sturdy two-wheeled horse-drawn cart to make his rounds and I was sometimes allowed to ride with him, which was a great treat. We travelled very fast over uneven fields and I was a little bit scared I would fall out, although I never admitted this to anyone in case they stopped me going. The estate had several horses, who seemed to me very big and a little scary, but very beautiful.

There was a lake near the big house, and we regularly took boats out with picnic baskets and played games on the other side of the lake. They bred pigeons and there was a big pigeon coop designed like a small house, which fascinated me. I loved watching the different-coloured birds with their iridescent sheen, strutting in and out of the little doors. Small children remember and are impressed by the oddest things: this family had the first English-style lavatory I had ever seen and I was mesmerised by it. German toilets have a ledge inside them, English ones go straight down to the water, so you get a splashing sound, which really impressed me. We called it a *Plumpsklo*. They were

idea how much it was, but it was a big win. Like a father in a fairy story, he gave his three daughters a share of his win, asking them all to choose something they would like. My mother chose very fine silver cutlery and Meissen china, which she loved, and other things she wanted for the house. Aunt Irma chose jewellery, because there was nothing else she needed. And Aunt Hilda, like the wise daughter in a story, chose a plot of land, which in the end, as we would discover, turned out to be the best option.

My grandfather always told me that I had inherited his luck. I'm still buying lottery tickets just in case!

In Hamburg, when I was growing up, my grandmother ran a sort of luncheon club for businessmen. They would come to her apartment for lunch each working day, so it was like a small restaurant, but it was not open to the public and she only served weekday meals. All her three daughters, my mother, my Aunt Hilda and my Aunt Irma, would help out, so I would go there too. I can remember Grandmother had a small table with little chairs for me and my cousin Volker,

Aunt Hilda's youngest son. Volker is only four weeks older than me, so we were like twins, and the two of us had to sit quietly, as the businessmen liked to discuss their affairs over their meals and did not want to be disturbed by young children. Our other cousin, Henning, Aunt Irma's only child, was also there, but only a baby at the time as he was four years younger than Volker and me. The family always told a joke about Henning's birth: Aunt Irma had been waiting so long for a baby that when my grandmother heard that she was pregnant at the age of forty she said, 'Don't be silly, don't listen to her. It is the change of life.' Aunt Irma's life certainly did change, but luckily it was with Henning.

———————

I have many memories of my life in the flat on the Wandsbecker Chaussee. The smell of baking bread still takes me right back there, because on the ground floor of our block was a bakery run by a family called Wedemeier and from very early in the morning the delicious aroma of baking bread would pervade the area. Sometimes Mutti would phone down and tell them what she wanted and I was allowed to go down on my own to collect it. Ours was a big, double-fronted apartment block with a sweeping staircase, which I would run down and then walk slowly back up, savouring the smell of the warm bread I was carrying. I was not allowed to use the lift without an accompanying adult.

Inside the flat we had a large living room, with double doors across one end, which closed off another room, the smoking room. This was effectively my father's study, where he kept all his books. He would retire into it to smoke and it was his own domain, a bit forbidden to the rest of us. There were long leather settees that seemed enormous to me and they were freezing cold on my little bare legs that poked straight out of my short skirts. But after a while, they'd warm up and stick to my skin.

At Christmas a tree would be smuggled into the smoking room, and the grown-ups would secretly decorate it and put the presents underneath. Then the doors would be firmly locked until Christmas Eve, which is the day of the great celebration in Germany. In the evening we would go to church and when we returned, the big folding doors would be opened and my father would ring a little bell.

worst was over and she was back home with us, convalescing. Only Ruth had escaped the infection.

Ruth was my beautiful, glamorous, ever-so-grown-up sister. At nineteen, she worked as a graphic designer in the city and had a busy social life. She was a member of a biking club and she loved the theatre. One night she was planning to go to the theatre with friends, but at the last minute she cried off. Her throat was sore – too sore for her to go out – and she decided to go to bed instead. Within a very short time she was extremely weak and they feared that she too had caught scarlet fever. But it wasn't the fever – something else had taken hold of her. The apartment was hushed, and the atmosphere tense and strained. The doctor came, but this time she did not come to see me.

Ruth was ill for only three days. Everyone was terribly concerned about her and she was about to be taken to hospital. The ambulance was on its way and had even arrived downstairs, but her throat was gradually closing until she could no longer breathe. She suddenly sat up, put her arms round our mother and in barely a whisper said, '*Oh, meine liebe Mutti*' – oh, my darling Mummy – and died.

Else, who lived near Berlin and was married to Uncle Artur. She refers to my sister as 'big Ruth', because Aunt Else had a daughter, also called Ruth, who was always known as 'little Ruth'. Little Ruth was just three weeks older than me and, like me, was a surprise unplanned baby, born after the others in the family were in their teens.

Dear Else and family

The first few days of this uncertain time have passed. For us, the loss of our beloved 'big' Ruth is still hard to believe. Her death came too quickly. Waldi had to go back to his post. He has been transferred so much further away. You can imagine how hard it was for him to return there.

Dear Else, you have a lot of troubles too. Please let me know very soon what is happening with Günther. I can't help thinking about you all.

Our Bärbel is in bed with scarlet fever. She is over the worst and can hopefully get up soon. Eva contracted scarlet fever at work and was in Mecklenburg Hospital for six weeks. She had just come home for convalescence here with us in Hamburg, so she was present when Ruth died. Ruth was only ill for three days. She felt very weak on Sunday evening. On Monday I called Doctor Wagner. She tested her for scarlet fever, which was negative. In the night from Tuesday to Wednesday Ruth was very poorly, so I called the doctor again on Wednesday morning. Ruth was supposed to be admitted to hospital at 3 p.m. with 'severe angina'.

As the ambulance men were bringing the stretcher up to the third floor Ruth suddenly sat up in bed, put her arms around me and said, 'My darling Mutti' and she was dead. I am still shaking when I relive these seconds. Our so industrious, ever-ready-to-help-out and so happy Ruth! It is awful. She died of diphtheria. We bought a beautiful plot at the cemetery at Ohlsdorf, a family resting place for all of us.

The funeral service was most beautiful. All that was dear to her we sent off with her. If she looked down she would have seen how much love and devotion everyone paid her on her last journey. The chapel could hardly contain all the mourners. So many flowers: Ruth always gave flowers to people and it seemed that people gave them all back to her in one lot.

Two days ago, on 8 April, Ruth would have been twenty years old. Our big Ruth, and now she is covered by cold earth. I don't think I will ever stop crying.

Dear Else and Artur, please reply to my letter very soon and tell me what is happening at yours – how is everyone keeping?

Your very sad sister-in-law Norma, Eva and Bärbel

With Ruth's death, our home was a different, much sadder place. A stranger came to the flat to look after me during the funeral, because I was still unwell and too young to go. She was a friend of my parents but I did not know her and it added to the feeling of everything being fractured in a way I did not comprehend. Then they came to fumigate the flat, to kill off any remaining infection, and I had to wear a mask while they did it.

We had to go on as best we could after Ruth had

died. After all, a great many tragedies were taking place all over the world and thousands, even millions, of people were losing loved ones in far worse circumstances. Nevertheless, a great sorrow filled our lives and I can remember the sadness of that time.

My mother coped by throwing herself into caring for Eva and me. We were both still poorly, recovering from our own bouts of scarlet fever, and my mother was selfless in her devotion to getting us better. Perhaps she was terrified at the thought that anything could go wrong with one of her two remaining daughters, or maybe it was her way of coping with the enormity and finality of Ruth's death. Whatever the reason, she worked tirelessly, constantly checking on us and ministering to us, and taking no account of herself or her own health. When Eva and I were both fully recovered, my mother's poor body finally rebelled and she collapsed. She was taken to hospital, paralysed and unable to walk. The doctors could find no reason for her paralysis and initially feared she would never walk again. Home was a strange place without my beloved Mutti, but she was gone and it looked as though it would be months before she returned home to us.

My sister Eva was doing her war work, which was compulsory for girls of her age. Before then, she had been a member of the Bund Deutscher Mädel, the League of German Girls, which was the equivalent of the Hitler Youth for boys. It was compulsory for everyone from ten to eighteen to belong to one of the two organisations, the BDM or the Hitler Youth. When they were initially set up, in the early thirties, the Hitler Youth attracted lots of boys because of its sporty outdoor 'Boy Scout' adventures, but very few girls volunteered for the BDM. Once Hitler had abolished all other youth organisations the ranks swelled and, with the increasing Nazification of Germany in the pre-war years, it became the acceptable thing to do. It provided an ordered social life for young people and no doubt lots of fun, with hikes and sing-songs and campfires. They learned dancing, cooking and needlework. Of course, it was all overlaid with Nazi indoctrination, but in those days most parents and children were oblivious to this. In 1936 it became obligatory to be a member and this was reinforced by law in 1939.

From 1943 onwards, girls of Eva's age were expected to do war work. Some of them worked as secretaries in military or government establishments, some manned anti-aircraft batteries, some even became soldiers and fought and died alongside men. Luckier ones were sent to work on farms, the equivalent of Britain's Land Army girls. Others, if they were intelligent and had some education, were assigned teaching jobs, educating the young girls of ten upwards who were evacuated to BDM homes in the countryside.

Eva was one of these. Although she was not qualified and was too young to have been to university, she was deemed able to teach the younger girls, so she was sent away to a BDM home as a teacher.

With Mutti ill and Eva away, there was nobody left at home in the Hamburg apartment to care for me, so I went to live with my father in Posen. I did not know it then, but I would never return to that apartment. My happy days on the Wandsbecker Chaussee were over for ever. I'm glad now that I lived in innocence and did not know that I was departing that life for good.

Because my father's work on the railways

involved travelling about, and because he was living on his own in the flat, I was billeted with a succession of his friends. My father was a very sociable man, always good company, and he had a wide circle of friends who were happy to take me in. I was well brought up, had good manners and I don't think it was hard for him to find people to look after me. First, I was with the Sundermanns, whom I already knew well and where there were my friends Heinz and Fritz. Then I stayed with other families with children of the same sort of age as me and, apart from missing my mother, I was well looked after and happy.

But not always. I have one miserable memory of that time. I was staying with a couple my father knew but whom I had never met before, a childless couple who had little understanding of small children. They had two German Shepherd dogs roaming free around their house, so when the woman put me to bed she told me there was a chamber pot under the bed for me if I needed a wee-wee in the night, as the dogs would prevent me going to the bathroom. I was five, I had not used a potty since I was a baby and I was scared of using one on my own. So I decided I would not use it, no matter what. Then, in the early hours of the morning, I did want to wee. I held it and held it, determined not to use the potty, but then I dropped off to sleep again and dreamed that I had found a toilet. What a great relief! I found it and was at last able to stop holding in so hard. There was a lovely feeling of relaxation and warmth. Of course, I woke to find I had wet the bed, something I had never done before. I was very ashamed, but nevertheless the woman looking after me was cruel, because she told everybody in the village what had happened. I was very unhappy and longed to go home. Oh, I wanted my Mutti, my own mummy! I can still remember that sensation of great relief.

My mother was ill for five or six months and after a while she was transferred from her hospital to a nursing home near to where I was living with my father. Although she was improving, she was still suffering from the paralysis that had come upon her so strangely. The only medical reason we were ever given for her condition was that it was to do with her nervous system: the acute psychological distress she was in had caused her body to refuse to obey. We visited her often and would take her into the grounds in her wheelchair, and our father would lift her on to a blanket on the grass and we would have a picnic. Gradually, she improved and at last she was able to move into the flat with my father and me, and we were reunited.

It seemed so terrible at the time, but actually my mother's illness and my evacuation to the Wartegau saved our lives.

2

A Peaceful Polish Interlude

On 25 July 1943, British and American bombs started to fall heavily on Hamburg. There had been bombing raids before, but nothing as intensive as this. Hamburg was a natural target because it was the second biggest German city, with a population of one and three-quarter million, and the biggest port in the country. It was an important industrial target for the Allies, as the city's shipyards were busy producing the U-boat submarines, averaging more than one a week for the two years before the raids. The city also had factories producing aircraft parts, lots of different engineering factories and vital oil refineries.

Even before we left, Hamburg had been attacked and, while I was too young to know why it was such a prime target, I certainly understood the words 'air raid'. The approach of the bombers would be announced by the howling of the air attack alarms and we would hurry down from our flat to the underground shelter beneath the apartment block. Almost every block had its own shelter and all the residents would huddle there together, waiting for the end of the raid before we ventured above to see what had happened. It seemed that we were lucky – our building always escaped serious damage.

But that July, two months before my sixth birthday while we were far away in Posen, the heavy raids began. In a few short days over 10,000 tons of bombs were dropped on the city. More than 500 British and Allied airmen died in the battle for Hamburg and approximately 44,600 German civilians died. Some were killed directly by the bombs but many more by the fires that raged through the buildings. Over half of all homes in the city were destroyed and 900,000 people were homeless. Many of them fled from the city. Remarkably, some train services were still running and fares were waived so that refugees travelled free. Others escaped as best they could, in horse-drawn carts or on foot.

The news came that the apartment block on the Wandsbecker Chaussee had suffered a direct hit and was destroyed. There was at first relief that we were safe – my father and mother, Eva and I – so we were very lucky indeed. But we had lost all our possessions except those we had with us. Perhaps the most difficult loss was of everything that had belonged to Ruth: that hit my mother much harder than the destruction of her other, more valuable, belongings.

It was an anxious time as we waited for news of what had happened to the rest of our family. Soon, we learned that my grandparents and my mother's two sisters, Aunt Hilda and Aunt Irma, and their children had also survived in underground shelters, but all three families had been bombed out of their homes. The husbands of both my aunts were away fighting and there had been no news of them for some time. Now they were all homeless and initially they stayed with other relatives who had homes in the suburbs that had escaped the raids. Then my father took charge and they all made their way to the Wartegau to join us. Through some good friends, a German family called Boetels who ran another large estate, my father knew of an empty house in the nearby tiny hamlet of Eulau, near the town of Punitz (Poniec). It was a large, one-storey building which had previously been the home of the manager of a brickworks. The brickworks had closed down and the house stood empty. It was set back from the road and behind it a track ran the 500 yards to the brick factory. My father set about taking it over and the whole family moved in.

It was a splendid and roomy house with four large bedrooms, which we called wings, all leading on to spacious communal rooms. My grandparents had one bedroom and each of the three sisters had her own room with her children. I don't know how they got there, but I can remember we all arrived at the same time and my father led my mother into the bedroom he had chosen for us. I have a vivid picture of each little family group sitting on the beds in their chosen room: there was no squabbling about who went where. Everyone was relieved and happy to have a solid roof over their heads, safely reunited.

We were all so glad to be together again, but it was not to last. One day a telegram arrived and after my mother had read it I heard her crying. It ordered my father to report to a certain depot at a certain time. She knew what it meant. His age, his injury and his important job could no longer save him. Germany was running short of conscripts for the army and men who had previously been excluded from service were now being called up. Soon, even the young boys would start to receive their papers to do their bit in the last struggles. My father was drafted to fight on the Russian Front. It was the worst possible news.

The grown-ups tried to keep their fears from me and told me that my father would be going away for a little while but that I was not to worry. To cheer me up and take my mind off his imminent departure, my parents took me to visit some friends whose dog, a dachshund, had just had a litter of puppies. I was thrilled with them and even more thrilled when, as we left, I was given a present of one of them. I called him Lumpie and he was adorable. As he got bigger he used to follow me everywhere.

With my father gone, we all got on with living

in our new home. Besides the four wings, there was a big living room with a *Kachelofen*, an oven built in to a high protruding section of the chimney breast, with a door at the front to put apples or potatoes in to bake. It was wood- and coal-fired, and was fed with fuel from the room behind. You simply shut down the fire to low at night and once a day emptied the ashes. Along the side of the oven, which was covered with shiny green ceramic tiles, was a bench where you could sit and toast yourself. There were also a dining room, a large kitchen and, at the back, a utility room and another kitchen, where we had a churn to make butter and cheese, and a special boiler for boiling sugar beet to make syrup. There was a further boiler for washing white clothes and a scrubbing board, and a large walk-in shower.

The house was comfortably furnished, which was fortunate as we had very few possessions. I had the clothes and toys my father had brought with me, and my mother had a little brown leather suitcase, which she had in hospital with her, with a soft towel and good soap, her underwear and nighties and dressing gown, and a set of silver cutlery she always carried. It was a tradition in our family that we all

lots of worms for them. We always nicknamed Ulrich 'the crazy one' but it was the aunts who went crazy when they saw the mess the birds made, and Ulrich was forced to release them and clean up.

Ulrich was eight years older than Volker and me, so he was naturally the leader of our little gang whenever he was around and often led us into mischief. He was very clever at persuading Volker and me to do what he told us. 'Bärbel is much braver than Volker!' he would declare. I liked this and, of course, to live up to it I had to agree to his games. Volker, too, would always agree, as he was keen to prove he was just as brave as me.

The old brickworks had a series of ponds next to it. They were man-made and were used to cool the hot, newly made bricks. The bricks would have been loaded into small railway trucks, which were then shunted down rails straight into the water. The rails and the trucks, which were big enough for us all to clamber into, still existed and we played with them endlessly. We were warned off by our mothers, especially after someone drowned in one of the further ponds, but under Ulrich's command we did it.

The factory itself was a three-storey building and

we roamed around inside. Ulrich told us there were foxes and that we could befriend them. In fact, I think the only creatures living there were probably rats and bats. One of the items of clothing my mother had brought with her was a fox fur stole, which she wore round her neck like a collar. It had the fox's head on one end and the long bushy tail at the other, which sounds gruesome but was very fashionable then. One day Ulrich told me to get the stole from the wardrobe in our bedroom, but not to tell anyone. He took it into the brickworks, hid it in a corner and tied a long piece of string to it. Then he took Volker, Henning and me on an adventure, and made us sit down in the same room as the hidden stole. As he cleverly pulled the string, the fox's head appeared, and Volker and Henning fled in fear. Mutti was not too happy when she found out: 'My beautiful stole on that filthy floor!' she said.

When Ulrich wasn't around, Volker, Henning and I were a great little team and we played together endlessly, occasionally getting into trouble. One day when the weather was bitterly cold the ditches around the farm fields were all frozen, and we three decided that if the ice was thick enough to support a stone, it would hold our weight. When the stone stayed on the surface, I was selected as the first to try my weight on the ice. I plunged straight up to my neck in icy water. Thank God, somebody was going past and hauled me out. I was not popular when I got home. My mother was obviously very worried that I could have drowned or frozen to death, but she was very cross with me, too, for being so stupid.

Eva and Thekla also visited us when they had leave from their teaching duties at the BDM homes. We were very excited when we knew they were coming and would run along the road to the turning for Poniec, to meet them as they walked from the train.

Next to our house was a courtyard and a small house where a Polish family lived. The mother used to help out in our house, and the father drove us in a horse and cart when we needed transport. Their son was younger than Volker and me, and he was not allowed to play in the brickworks, but he joined in our games in the courtyard. His name was Polish for Peter, so we always called him Peter. I even learned to speak a little Polish, but all I can remember after all these years is *mleko* (milk) and *daja mnie pocałunek* (give me a kiss).

Besides the marvellous playtimes we had, there were lessons too. Our parents were not going to allow us to neglect our education because there was a war going on. The people who had found the house for us, Mr and Mrs Boetels, had a tutor for their three children, so for a while we went up to the big manor house to share tuition. Later, perhaps because the tutor left, or because the family wanted to integrate more with local people, we were taken to a small school about two miles away. Every morning a lovely little horse-drawn carriage from the big house would collect me and Volker (Henning was too young for school). We felt ever so grand riding in it. I can't remember learning anything at the school, but I loved the journeys. Sometimes we would persuade the driver to stop and let us pick mushrooms on the way home.

The grown-ups also taught us. My mother had herself been a student at the prestigious Froebel Institute and had worked as a governess before she married, so she took charge of teaching Volker and me to read. Aunt Hilda had been what today is called a graphic designer, doing artwork for big businesses. She had beautiful handwriting and she made us write out line after line of letters. Aunt Irma taught me embroidery, and Grandmother taught me to knit and crochet. I remember sitting on her lap as she showed me the stitches. Little as I was, she always talked to me as if I were mature.

She passed on to me her own philosophy of life and it has served me well. 'Whatever you do, you don't have to run to church every day or every week. As long as you can put your head on your pillow at night and not be sorry for anything you have done during that day, that is what being a good Christian is about.' I have heard her voice in my head many times, reminding me, 'If you are going to have to say sorry, don't do it.'

There was one occasion when I was naughty and had to say sorry to my grandmother. She had a blouse with a lace collar, which was fastened all the way up with press-studs. Sometimes she had trouble doing it up, as her fingers were stiff. One day, while I sat on her lap, I pulled it all open. I was fascinated by the press-studs and wanted to see them pop open. But of course, as her blouse opened I saw her underwear. She was old-fashioned and very proper and private about things like that, and I felt so ashamed of what I had done. I can still recall the feeling of prickly embarrassment, but I can also remember seeing the most beautiful cream-coloured vest trimmed with lace that she had made herself. It was like the camisoles that young girls wear today. Omi did not really get angry with me, but I knew she did not like it. That night I said I was sorry in my prayers, and the next day I gave her a big hug and told her I would never do it again. She forgave me, of course.

I think we enjoyed Opa's lessons the most. He had been at sea for many years and he had won-derful stories to tell us about foreign countries. We had a globe with a light inside it – I've no idea how we came to have such a thing. He would plug it in and we would all crowd round him, near the warm stove in the living room. 'Where are we travelling today?' he would ask and we would roam the world with him, hanging on every word.

The women were all very good cooks and I learned from them too about how to run the house and conjure up delicious meals. There must have been food shortages, but we were protected from them and I was never aware of lacking anything. There was always something to eat on the table. I'm sure the three sisters and my grandmother had to be very resourceful, but we children took it as normal. The house we lived in had a garden full of fruit trees – apples, pears and many others – and there was a vegetable plot where we grew food. Despite the war raging around us, the most traumatic event for me in those blissful months was lightning striking our beautiful pear tree and splitting it in half. Luckily, one half continued to bear fruit. On the front of the house, growing up trellises, were grapevines, and I could reach out of our bedroom window and pick grapes.

Every time the big farm sent deliveries of produce to the market, their lorry would drop off a large wooden box in the entrance hall to our house (which was never locked) at six o'clock in the morning, full of tomatoes, celery, swedes and potatoes. I can remember the lovely smell of the fresh tomatoes and the taste when I helped myself to one.

My father had arranged the deliveries before he

left, and we always had money to pay for them and to pay the Polish family for their help. We had a bank account in Poniec, a thriving town with shops that could supply most things. Because we lived a few miles away from the town, we always had plenty of cash in the house.

While Father was still with us we had a supply of meat from his hunting. He went on organised shoots, and came back with rabbits and pheasants for us.

Sometimes we were all invited to a local farm for the '*schlachtfest*', or slaughter festival. It was the three or four days of the year when the farmer would employ slaughter men to kill the cattle and pigs that had been reared for their meat. Of course, we never saw the gruesome reality of the kill, but the whole event was turned into a big celebration, with spit roasted pigs and huge barbecues of steaks, chops, and sausages. There were tables laden with potatoes, salads, bread and butter, and lots to drink. We sat at trestle tables and benches, tucking in to the food, and then we children spilled around the farm, laughing and playing games together. There were demonstrations of sausage making, and the grown-ups would order the meat and sausages they wanted to buy. The supplies would last us for weeks.

We kept our own goat, which provided us with milk, and we also had cows' milk delivered from the big house. We made our own butter, the grown-ups sitting around passing the churn from one to another as their arms became tired. We grew sugar beets and boiled them in the small back kitchen to make a syrup, which we used to sweeten things. The smell of boiling beets is another powerful memory. It was a very self-sufficient, happy life. I have since learned that we were incredibly lucky. In Europe's big cities food was scarce and rationing severe. But if you lived in the country, as we did, things were relatively easy and we always seemed to eat well.

We lived in our large and comfortable home for eighteen months and life seemed almost normal. At one point I developed a growth behind my left knee and I was taken in the carriage from the big house to the nearest hospital, in Poniec, to have it removed. It has never troubled me since, but for several weeks I was in a plaster cast from my thigh to my toes, because the scar had to be stretched

3

The War Draws Closer

A few days after my grandfather's party, Eva was asked to report to Weimar, a city about 150 miles south of Hamburg. She was to meet up with the woman who was in charge of the evacuation of BDM girls to that region and receive further orders.

It was sad to say goodbye to Eva again, especially after we had had such a wonderful family celebration. She recorded in her diary that grandfather's birthday was 'a very special day' and wrote of our house near the brick factory as 'home', although she had never lived there full time. With the destruction of our flat in Hamburg it was the only home any of us had.

Eva went at once to Weimar as instructed, and there she was told to report that day to Tabarz, a small village near the city of Gotha, a few miles further south, in the region of Thuringia, which is renowned for its beauty. There was a home there for children sent to the countryside, the equivalent of British evacuees. She went straight away, travelling by two trains, and when she arrived at the station at Tabarz she was met by four of the ten-year-old girls who would be her charges and one of the women who worked at the home.

She described her new post in her diary:

The house is situated in a very beautiful road looking out on to woods. There is a lovely view over the Thuringian countryside. I am in charge of a group of ten-year-old girls. They are very young and still like to play, and it is easy to get them interested in things.

Her diary entries describe the routines of life in the home. Despite the war and a country drained by years of fighting, children were still children and for the girls in Eva's charge, just like me and my cousins in the Wartegau, life was made as normal as possible. There were celebrations of St Nicholas Day on 6 December. On the evening before children would leave shoes or slippers outside their bedroom doors. St Nicholas, who is a helper of Father Christmas, visits in the night and if they have been good they are rewarded with sweets or chocolates in the shoes. If they have been naughty they are given a small broom made of twigs, the kind of thing that is used to sweep or to beat carpets. It is meant to be a warning: if you don't improve you will get a good hiding.

Eva included a little verse in her diary that day, probably something given to all leaders in the BDM movement:

Our task is to guide the youth to go
straight and aim for the finish;
The big finish is to win the war and
be at peace.

Eva also recorded that rehearsals had started for the Christmas panto and she describes a St Martin's celebration when all the girls processed through the house with flaming torches, which is possibly a local tradition as I never did this myself.

So, in the midst of war, these festivals were maintained and the routines of everyday life were preserved for the young girls, even though they often had to spend their nights in the cellars because of what Eva describes as 'vicious' air raids.

She copied out a poem about the bombing of the big cities. Eva lost six of her friends in the raids on Hamburg, all young women doing the same job as her, teaching groups of young girls. One of the six, Magda, was a particular friend of hers, even though she was six years older than Eva and already married. They had a large funeral which Eva was unable to attend, but our mother went. Eva pasted into her diary a newspaper report of their funerals, on which is written in our mother's handwriting 'These also died for Germany'.

The poem about the bombing of Germany that appears in Eva's diary is called 'Köln. Allerseelen 1944'

('Cologne. All souls 1944') and was written by Otto
Brües. It begins:

> we have now left our house,
> It became a ruin, brick by brick,
> And this destroyed the parents' pride,
> the children's happiness.

The verses describe neighbours scrabbling to collect
possessions from the rubble, watching their past
lives disappear.

She also wrote out another poem, 'The Dream',
which starts:

> Last night I found great happiness
> I dreamed we were at peace.

The poem describes a world where the shops are full
of supplies and the bars are stocked with drink, and
everyone in the streets is happy. It is, of course, only
a dream and the writer is awakened to another air
raid. Eva wrote poetry herself, as well as collecting
other poems that she loved. As there is no name of
an author on this one, I wonder if it is one of hers.

I like to think it is. I know, from the other entries she made in her diary, that she did dream of peace.

———————

Nothing could stop the war advancing upon us. It was now the winter of 1944 and defeat was staring Germany in the face, although not everyone, including Hitler and his High Command, could accept it. My family had never been Nazi supporters, but they were loyal German citizens. My mother and both her sisters had husbands away fighting: they prayed for the war to end and for our families to be restored to normality. I don't think they prayed for a German victory. What they wanted was peace and a safe world to bring us up in.

The British, Americans and Russians were now pressing in on Germany. The Russians were moving the fastest and they were to prove by far the most ruthless. We were afraid of them, but we were also afraid of all the conquering armies. We had no idea how we would be treated. In June 1944 the Red Army swept into Romania, Bulgaria, Hungary and Poland. At roughly the same time the British and Americans launched the D-Day landings and were progressing across France and Holland towards Germany. It was a pincer movement and the Germans were effectively trapped.

Despite the disastrous circumstances that led us to be in Poland, life for us children was idyllic. We were unconcerned with the war, although I was aware that the women would weep at times, and occasionally we would hear the sound of planes, lots of them, high in the sky, a monotonous droning sound. We all ran out to see whether they were heading towards Russia. We would crane our necks to watch them and I once toppled over backwards into the grass because I was straining my head so far back. The direction meant nothing to me, but it was what the grown-ups did, so I followed suit. They encouraged us to wave at the planes: they did everything possible to shield us from the realities of war and waving at the planes made it seem like fun.

We had a radio and I know the grown-ups followed the progress of the war from the German news transmissions, which tended to emphasise German successes. But mostly the radio was tuned into music, which we all loved.

As defeat loomed ever closer, though, the adults

in our little commune obviously knew some of what was happening. They realised that the Russians were advancing through Poland towards us and that we were sitting in the path of an invading army. Nevertheless, they still hid their worries from us.

Christmas 1944 was as cheerful as they could make it. We had a Christmas tree with home-made decorations and we gave each other little presents we had made. We had small weaving looms, which Grandfather had made for us, and we wove the fabric for pincushions and pot holders, and we made bookmarks, which we decorated with pressed flowers and pretty ribbons. Because we lived in the countryside and food was relatively plentiful, we were fortunate to be able to celebrate in traditional style. We had a typical German Christmas meal with three geese because there were so many of us. When the giblets of the geese were boiled for broth and the gravy, Volker, Henning and I were each given the cooked heart of a goose to eat, because we were told that eating the goose heart would make our own hearts stronger. We had red cabbage and all the trimmings, and afterwards Stollen

(German Christmas bread) and poppy-seed cake. We children baked lots of the traditional Christmas biscuits.

I made a special Christmas card, which I sent to Eva. I drew candles and baubles and wrote, 'Dear Eva, I wish you a beautiful Christmas holiday, your Bärbel.' Far away in Tabarz, Eva pasted it into her diary and wrote underneath it, 'The little one's first letter.' In the BDM home, she too celebrated as best she could what she called the 'war Christmas, 1944'.

Eva's diary for the first few days of the New Year is a mixture of happy times – she writes about taking the young girls in her class skating, and reading them stories about the Snow Queen and the Little Mermaid – and her deeper concerns about the world:

My wish for the New Year is that now I will soon be reunited with my family. I hope life is going to be better for us than the last few years. Let's hope that the long-awaited peace will come and reunite us all in Hamburg.

She writes about her own dreams and longings:

> All I want is to be married with children, and have a little house and garden with flowers. I will be a good wife and do everything to make my husband feel wanted and special. What in the world could be nicer than that? I can't wait for the day when it might happen. But who knows what will happen in these hard and difficult times.

Her dreams were the same as those of many nineteen-year-old girls. She even drew a picture of a cradle with a baby in it and copied into her diary the words of a favourite lullaby, which she sang to me many times:

> Little child of mine, go to sleep.
> Because the stars are in the sky,
> And the moon is also coming,
> I will rock you in your cradle.
> Go to sleep, my little child, go
> to sleep.

Then the reality of the situation we were all in was brought home to her when, on 20 January 1945, the erratic postal service brought a letter from my mother. It asked Eva to come at once to fetch me away from the Wartegau.

Warsaw in Poland had already been attacked, she told Eva (the Russians took it on 17 January) and the fighting was moving closer to us all the time. My mother wanted to make sure that I, at least, was well away from the Russian advance. She felt that I would be safer with Eva in Tabarz.

Eva wrote:

Mutti said I should come and get Puppe, as the danger from the East is growing, with big attacks. I was still wearing my ski outfit and I went immediately, dressed as I was. By 11 p.m. in the evening I got to Leipzig, but then I couldn't go on because there was no train to Dresden. The next morning I continued and got as far as Aunt Else [near Berlin]. I saw tracks and tracks of wagons trying to get to the west. I met a woman who had just lost her twins through starvation and hunger. She was so upset, I felt so sorry for her. The attacks were so fierce from the low-flying planes, and there were grenades exploding around me, I was really lucky not to be hit. There was no way I could get to Rawitsch (in Polish Rowicz, the town in the Wartegau where she could have caught a connecting train for Poniec) so I had to turn round. The shooting was absolutely incredible. I was so tired I could not go on and I had to spend one night in the waiting room of a train station.

It took her seven days altogether to get back to Tabarz. It was a harrowing and fruitless journey for her, and when I look back now my heart breaks to think that she risked so much for me. But there was one very positive outcome from her trip. When she met up with my father's sister, Aunt Else, she was given three very precious possessions, which I now have. Everything that we ever owned of Ruth's was destroyed in the bombing of our flat, but Aunt Else had the handwritten announcement of her death, which my mother had sent out, along with Mutti's letter about her death and, most poignantly, a postcard that Ruth herself had written. The content is banal enough: Ruth sends her greetings, promises to come and visit soon, and asks about Aunt Else's husband and children, Günther, Heinz, Horst and Ruth. It is addressed to Aunt Else and 'little Ruth'. She ends with 'A thousand kisses and greetings, Ruth'. But to see her handwriting and to have something that she touched is very precious.

Eva wrote in her diary:

If I read through them the tears come, but I must admit to myself that Ruth is possibly the best off out of all of us. She does not have to go through this horrible war, which has robbed us of everything. She does not have to go through what we are all experiencing. I ask myself all

the time what did we do to deserve
this. But we can't change it. we have
to carry on and make the best of
it.

Before Eva made it back to Tabarz, my mother, my aunts and my grandparents realised she could not get through to rescue me. The Wartegau was becoming a very dangerous place to be. The time had come to shatter the idyll: we had to flee in the path of the invading Russians.

This was when my first big adventure of the war began. The war ceased to be a strange, abstract thing that preoccupied the grown-ups and became my reality. There was no way to shelter us from it any longer. For the next few months I was truly a child of war.

When Mr and Mrs Boetels up at the manor house heard that everyone had to leave, they sent a Polish driver to warn us and to tell us to pack up at once. We would be picked up in six hours' time. But rather than worry about the three German sisters and their little children, the driver decided he needed to get home to his own family, who were as much at risk as we were from the marauding Russian troops. He never came to give us the message. In the turmoil of everything that was going on, I cannot blame him.

What I can never forgive, though, is the action of some of the other Polish workers on the large estate. As fear and panic broke out, one of them shot Mr Boetels. It was, I suppose, a reaction against the Germans who had colonised their land, some of whom had acted with horrific cruelty, although we knew nothing of that at the time. Mr Boetels was not like that at all. He was not responsible for the actions of the German High Command and he was a kind man who took great care of the Poles who worked for him. Some of the other workers knew this and they helped his wife hurriedly dig a shallow grave. She was not allowed the luxury of grieving for him – she, like us, had to start out on the trek back to Germany. There was no time to be lost.

The very first thing we knew about the evacuation was when a cart pulled by four horses arrived to collect us, sent by Mrs Boetels. It was a shock. We had spent the bitterly cold January day tucked up warm in our comfortable house, never thinking that we should have been making preparations for the flight.

It was a big open cart, usually used to transport milk churns, with room on it for the eight of us and covered with hay for us to sit on. We had to set off immediately, so we scooped together some essentials for the journey. It was a bitingly cold winter, so we children were all dressed in several layers of clothing. I wore thick woollen stockings knitted by my grandmother and attached to buttons on a crocheted camisole I had on over my vest. On top were trousers and several jumpers, and we took loads of blankets. I had to run round to the home of the Polish family who lived near us and give my darling puppy Lumpie to Peter, their son. It was a sad parting, but there was no time to linger and, besides, I really felt I would be back soon to collect him. We children understood that we were fleeing from the Russians, and that they were our enemies and bad men we should fear, but nothing more.

Sacks of food were thrown into the hay, but it was done so hurriedly that what we thought was a hundredweight of dried peas turned out to be a sack full of salt – a godsend, as it later turned out, for clearing the ice under the feet of the horses. Mutti had her little leather suitcase, which she took every-where, so her cutlery survived and so did our photo album.

We all climbed aboard to begin our journey. Grandmother refused to flop down in the hay with the rest of us, and one of the dining-room chairs was hastily brought and put on the back of the cart. She insisted on travelling backwards, so that she did not have to look at the rear end of the horses. She looked very regal, sitting up there with a beautiful, big, black straw hat on her head. The hat was another example of the resourcefulness of the womenfolk – Grandmother had made it and had lacquered it black. Unfortunately, it was not designed to be worn in the snow that was soon falling on us and the lacquer began to run. Grandmother sat perfectly still, trying to preserve her dignity, with black streaks running down her face. My mother removed the hat and tied a shawl round her, such as the rest of us were wearing. We also had umbrellas and must have looked an odd sight, all of us piled on the back of a haycart with umbrellas shielding us from the snow.

There were four horses pulling us and one of the employees from the manor house was driving. We rapidly joined up with the rest of the convoy, which included Mrs Boetels and her family.

It did not occur to me to wonder where Mr Boetels was – I assumed that he was staying behind to run the farm. We children were not told of his death until later and I was very sad to hear of it. I had liked him very much; he was a friendly, generous man who had taken good care of my family after Father went into the army. He certainly did not deserve his fate.

There were eight or ten large wagons, all rumbling west towards the German border almost 200 miles away, with a contingent of spare horses so that we could change them over when they were tired. Again, another smell drifts back through my memory, the smell of the nosebags of oats and hay that the horses wore to stop them spilling any valuable food. It smelled like wet, newly mown grass.

The milk wagon had rubber rims to its wheels, which were not good on snow, and the roads were made of large paving slabs with cracks, which could cause the wheels to lock and skid. There were many times when we all felt we were going to be pitched over into the snow.

It was impossible to hold up the convoy for toilet breaks, and we became adept at jumping down, scurrying into the bushes and running to catch up with the carts. Progress was slow and it was possible even for my short legs to run faster than the carts were moving. Little Henning was too small to jump off. He was wearing a little leather fur-lined hat with ear flaps, like a Sherlock Holmes hat, and when he announced that he needed a wee, Grandmother told him that he would have to turn his hat inside out and wee into it. He was very indignant and refused. In the end, one of the grown-ups held him over the side of the cart. To this day, even though he is now a man in his sixties, we tease him that he is going to have to wee in his hat.

The Boetels family had covered coaches, the smart, varnished vehicles that had ferried us to and from school, and around the countryside. They were luxurious, with lanterns outside, plush seats, and steps for mounting and dismounting. The grown-ups quickly arranged for Grandmother and Grandfather to travel under cover, and eventually we were all in the covered coaches and our milk cart was used just to transport our belongings. We had to make such good speed that we travelled day and night, sleeping huddled together in blankets. The drivers sat outside up high on the covered coaches, and they were wrapped in layers of blankets, with fur hats pulled over their heads. I cannot recall whether they were Polish or German, but I remember chattering to them when we were allowed to sit outside with them if it was sunny. Sometimes we would be permitted to hold the reins, which was very exciting.

We rumbled onwards through the blackest of nights. Even the towns and villages were in darkness: there were no street lights and the houses were all blacked out. We seemed to be travelling endlessly under a very big, starry sky. In daylight, as we came into towns and villages, there were soup kitchens set up in schools or community halls, organised by the local mayors and welfare groups. Sometimes we would get leek and potato soup or pea and potato soup. Often it was clear broth, just made from stock. It all tasted delicious and we were very grateful. We had no time to stop and cook for ourselves. We had taken bread with us, which was getting harder and harder as the days progressed. The grown-ups told us to chew it very well before swallowing it. Best of all was to soften it with the broth, which made a good, warming meal. I can still picture the steam coming off those wonderful bowls of soup, which were served to us in metal dishes we brought with us. We would stamp our feet on the cobbles to warm them up, trying at the same time not to spill a drop of our desperately needed hot soup.

Sometimes, when the convoy paused, we would feed the horses precious apples and carrots from our own supplies, to show them how grateful we were to them for pulling us. One of the grown-ups showed me how to hold out my hand flat with the treat on it and I can still remember the feel of the hairy wet lips of the horse as it snuffled up the food.

There were many other convoys on the road and often we would be in a huge stream of vehicles. There were no cars or lorries, as they had been commandeered by the army and, besides, there was no fuel. Sometimes the columns of carts would grind to a halt because one up at the front had broken an axle or overturned in the snow, and all the drivers would leap down to help. The organisation was very efficient. As soon as we reached a small town or village, we would be directed to separate soup kitchens. Then, when we took to the road again, the different convoys would be given different routes, presumably so that we did not all crowd together at the same bridge. Some of the volunteers who helped feed the convoys were Polish, others were Germans who had lived in the Wartegau all their lives and did not want to move, despite the Russian threat. For us, who had only been there eighteen months, the decision to leave was easy. For others it must have been very hard. I fear that those Germans who decided to stay lived to regret that decision.

We made steady progress and there were never any long hold-ups on the road, although we were limited by the pace of the long-suffering horses. If the adults were worried that we would not make the bridges in time, they did not show it, keeping us amused by getting us to sing songs and play word games. We must have been on the road for three days or so when we came to the bridge across the River Oder, the first of the two mighty rivers that form a natural barrier between Poland and Germany. We crossed near the town of Glogau (Glogów). Between the two rivers we stopped in the town of Sprottau (Szprotawa) and it was from there that Eva, down in Tabarz, received a postcard from Mutti to say that we were on our trek.

Eva wrote in her diary:

I am so happy to have finally received a message from her. So I know now that the Russians will not catch up with them. Mutti knows nothing about Father. We just hope and pray that he will get through all right, and that soon we will have a letter from him. I am so happy that Mutti and Bärbel and all the relatives are OK.

It was night-time when we reached the second bridge, across the Neisse at Cottbus. At last, we were almost home. The convoys had made their journey successfully and it seemed that we were safely back. There were a great many German soldiers around, urgently directing us to keep moving and get across because they were waiting to set the explosives and demolish the bridge.

Finally we rumbled across and when we reached the other side, everyone cheered and started singing, but we could not stop as we had to clear the area as soon as possible. Before we were a mile or two down the road we heard a huge explosion, and I looked back and saw the sky lit up with an enormous orange glow. They had blown up the bridges and we had made it across only by minutes. I heard later that those who arrived too late were ferried across the rivers in boats, but that meant they had to leave their few possessions behind. Even that was far better than facing the marauding Russian army.

On 25 January, as we were reaching German soil, there was fierce fighting in the streets of Posen, close to where we had been living. The Germans were defeated by the might and manpower of the Red Army, and the German civilians who were still there were subjected to terrible treatment, especially the women. Our escape had literally been in the nick of time and, although we children did not understand it all, we shared the huge sense of relief and celebration that swept through the long chain of carriages and carts as we travelled towards safety and away from the ruin of the two bridges that had carried us back home.

Our convoy rolled on for the rest of that night and the whole of the next day, until we reached the small village of Wiedersdorf, near Halle. Halle is a big city, the capital of the salt area of Germany, famous as the birthplace of Handel. It is a medieval city that was largely undamaged by the war. We stopped before we reached the city walls, our convoy being pulled over at Wiedersdorf. The welfare organisation was still working magnificently and this tiny village of less than 1,000 inhabitants had its doors open to welcome refugees. We had travelled about 160 miles, in appalling weather, but at least we were safely back in Germany.

Mrs Boetels and her family now went their separate way, pressing on in their carriages. They had a home south of Hamburg and I think they made their way there. I know that my parents kept in touch with Mrs Boetels until her death, but I don't recollect ever seeing the family again. In wartime, everyone tried to help each other, but nevertheless I will always be grateful to them for their particular kindness to us.

As we parted from them, we were taken in by another, equally kind, family. I cannot remember their names, but it was a school headmaster and his wife. All the three sisters, Aunt Irma, Aunt Hilda and Mutti, each with a small child, were billeted with them. Our grandparents were across the road with another family. It was blissful to be in a proper bed again and I think I slept for a long time on my first night in Wiedersdorf.

For a few days, Eva had no idea where we were. She rang a cousin of ours, but they had no news of us. She wrote in her diary:

where can everybody be? I am so terribly unhappy. I hope I get some good news from someone.

A couple of days later she pasted two photographs into her diary, pictures of herself in her skiing clothes and of her sitting on the edge of a field.

Today I am putting two photos in my diary from my time here in Tabarz. Since these were taken, a lot has happened. I made a journey to the East to help my family but did not get through to our house because the bombing was so bad that I had to turn back. Nobody was allowed any further. But I do know that they all got out OK. My dear father is somewhere, fighting. I know he is a soldier at heart and will do his best. I trust that an end to this war is in sight. Surely such a good, hard-working country cannot go under.

headmaster and his wife had a cellar lined with shelves full of apples and pears stored in tissue paper, along with stacks of jars filled with home-made jams, and preserved fruit and vegetables from the garden. On one special occasion the headmaster took us three children down there and allowed us to choose an apple or a pear each. The smell of that cellar is something I will never forget – it was full of such a lovely fragrance of fruit.

Our kind hosts gave us a belated Christmas meal, again the traditional German goose and red cabbage. They kept their own chickens and a couple of geese. Beforehand, we children were allowed to bake biscuits, which we cut into the shape of stars and moons. They had some icing sugar and we iced them half in white and half in pink. We also baked gingerbread men, with currants for their eyes and nuts for their noses, and again, the aroma of fresh gingerbread triggers my memories of that time.

I think they fed us well, but perhaps my memories are rose-tinted, because I do know that on one occasion my mother and my two aunts stole one of their chickens, in order to cook it for us. We children were all asleep, but we heard the story later and over the years it became one of our favourite family tales. The three sisters managed to round up the chicken and get it into the house, but they could not catch it to kill it. The more they tried, the more it squawked and cackled around the kitchen, and they were frightened of waking the owners. At one point they tried to give it some alcohol, in the hope that if it was drunk it would quieten down and fall asleep. In the end, they had to chase it out of the house again, after they decided that none of them had the stomach to kill it anyway. But it gave them all a good laugh. The chicken was even given a name, Mesimeco, which is an amalgam of the first letters of all our surnames.

It seemed we were now settled in Wiedersdorf and soon I was beginning to feel safe. The images of the fierce bad Russians, which had been so vivid as we fled from Poland, were fading in my imagination. My mother, though, knew that the situation was far from safe and she wrote to Eva again, asking her to come and collect me and take me back with her to Tabarz.

Eva agreed and set off at once. This journey was much easier than her last attempt. The trains were still running, and she took one from Gotha to Leipzig and another to Halle. I was thrilled to see her and so happy that she was going to stay with us for a few days at the house of the headmaster and his wife, who seemed glad to accept yet another member of the family.

My mother took me aside quietly to explain what was happening. 'Now, Puppe,' she said. 'You are going to go and stay with Eva for a while. Won't that be lovely? It will be a nice little holiday for you. Imagine – there will be lots of girls for you to play with and they all have so much fun. They go tobogganing, and skating and walking, and you will be able join in. Won't you like that?'

'Oh, yes!' I was delighted at the thought of going away with my big sister, to take part in all the activities she told me about with the girls in Tabarz. And life in the headmaster's house was not always comfortable as there were so many of us that it was cramped and restricted. We were aware that we always had to be on our best behaviour and not make any noise – I don't think the headmaster ever shouted at us, but he was a rather awe-inspiring figure. The grown-ups, too, were conscious of being guests in someone else's home and kept us in check. Mutti and Eva made Tabarz sound so exciting that I longed to go there.

When the time came to leave, I was not too upset about saying goodbye to Mutti; I was so pleased to be going with my big sister for our thrilling trip.

'Goodbye, my little Bärbel,' she said, kissing me. 'This is a small present for you, to remember your Mutti by.'

It was a pretty little pink blanket, just for me. Then, when I realised that I would really be leaving, I *was* sad. How could I leave my own Mutti? I didn't want to go, but they told me it would only be for a short time, and the prospect ahead of me was like a wonderful holiday.

As Eva and I waved farewell to Mutti, we did not know how long it would be or what we would go through before we would see her again.

———

We travelled by train. I don't remember too much about the main part of the journey, except sitting on the train with Eva, looking out of the window at the countryside rolling past. But I have very clear memories of the last bit of the journey, from Gotha to Tabarz. Gotha is a famous old European city: the British royal family used the name Saxe-Coburg-Gotha until the First World War, when they changed it to Windsor because it sounded less German. The Almanack of Gotha is the bible of European aristocracy, and there is an impressive palace in the city. But we were not sightseeing. Although the city was undamaged by bombs, Eva's main concern was to get me safely to the home at Tabarz and the way to do this was by a picturesque mini-train that ran through the Thuringian forest. The little forest train, or Thüringerwaldbahn, took sixty minutes to make what I thought was a magical journey.

We trundled past the palace of Reinhardsbrunn, the hunting seat of the Dukes of Gotha, where Queen Victoria loved to spend her summers, and through the village of Friedrichroda to Tabarz. The train had a bell, which would ring as it neared each tiny station. To me, it was like travelling on a toy train. The trees in the forest were laden with snow, and everything around us was breathtakingly white and sparkling.

The train stopped near the home and the tinkle of the bell could be heard from there. Whenever visitors were expected, and the bell sounded, the girls would run down to meet the train. Some were there to greet Eva and me when we arrived, as Eva was popular, and the girls and the staff missed her when she was away.

They had been waiting for my arrival with some excitement. When Eva failed to collect me on her first attempt they were very disappointed, especially as they had prepared a special present for me. They had made me a large rag doll. Once Eva and I had been taken up to the home and welcomed in, they presented her to me. I was delighted and instantly named her Charlotte. She was beautiful, the most beautiful doll any child has ever had. She was about twelve inches high, and was wearing a purple and red velvet trouser suit, with a hood from which some fair woollen curls protruded. Her features had been embroidered on in a smile. They had also made her a cradle and a padded sleeping bag. I loved my Charlotte and carried her everywhere with me. She and I slept together in a small bed in Eva's room with my pink blanket tucked round us, and I cuddled her while Eva read me stories, sang lullabies and said my prayers with me every night.

I was also given a tiny wooden toy train with five carriages and one engine, to remind me of the little forest train I had arrived on. The woman in charge of the home, Miss Ramelow, gave it to me and I kept it at the side of my bed. There were other toys in the home, but these were my own special ones, the only ones I had, as everything had been left behind when we fled from Poland, or was destroyed in the bombing of Hamburg.

There were about fifty girls living at the home. Eva's group, the youngest, were all ten, but there were also some older girls. They were in the BDM and they had been evacuated from big cities to keep them safe from the bombs. I fitted in to life in the home without too much trouble. I went to lessons and, although I was three years younger than the other girls, I could follow a lot of what they were being taught. I loved the poetry, drawing and home economics classes, and maths was one of my favourites. There was a strict routine. Eva would be awakened at 6 a.m. and get herself ready, then she would wake the girls, and inspect their beds, cupboards, fingernails and hair. After breakfast there would be a short assembly, and we always said a prayer for those who had died and those who were still fighting. I would close my eyes especially tight at this bit and think of my father, willing him to be alive and to come home. One of the staff would give an interesting short talk; Eva gave one about the life of Schiller, the great German poet and writer. Then we went to lessons and followed the rest of the school day. I think it was probably very similar to life in an English boarding school.

As well as lessons there was plenty of fun. It was hard to remember that there was a war on sometimes, as life seemed so carefree and normal. Eva's diary is full of tales of walks, slides they made on the ice, tobogganing, skating and skiing. When school work and chores like cleaning and darning socks were over, the girls had film shows on a screen, and they were always busy making things and preparing little plays to perform. Whenever a member of staff had a birthday, the girls would put on a small show that they devised themselves.

I was given a part in a show they were preparing

do. Actually, I could stay here — I'm sure no policeman will make me walk on. And down in Tabarz no one will open their doors for me at this time of night. Well, then. Goodnight!

So, with a big yawn, the traveller made a bed in the forest and lay down to sleep, and in the night the elves and little animals came and danced around. I loved being allowed to take part with the big girls.

The home had originally been a large manor house and there was a gong in the hall. It was struck to call us to meals, but it was also banged rapidly and hard when there was an air raid warning and we all had to go to the cellars. Sometimes we went three or four times a night.

I adored being with Eva. The girls all seemed to love her and I was so proud to be her sister. She was my idol — all I wanted was to grow up and be like her. The fact that Ruth had gone made her all the more precious to me. While I was there we had the second anniversary of Ruth's death. Eva never showed me how low and worried she was, but she wrote in her diary:

This is not a very good time, but we will plod on. Sometimes I am so upset that I don't know what to do next. Sorry, I shouldn't be so weak. I just don't understand the world any more. Sometimes I wish I had never been born. How will everything end?

She knew by this time that the American and British troops were already over the Rhine and sweeping up through Germany. The blowing up of the Rhine bridges had temporarily halted them, but by 7 March, a month before our journey began, they were across the river. By the final week of March they had completely taken the eastern bank of the river and were at Düsseldorf, less than 150 miles away from us. Everyone was very afraid, although, as before, I was protected from this as much as possible. But the adults all believed that the Americans would starve us out, surrounding villages like Tabarz and cutting off all supplies until everyone was dead. We expected them to be monsters, who would behave viciously and without mercy towards us. It was what we had been told endlessly by the Nazi propaganda machine.

When she heard these awful stories of the fate that awaited us all, Eva made an important decision. It was very likely, she thought, that we were going to die. And if that was the case, she wanted us both to be with our mother at the end so that we could all die together.

One evening, Eva took me into our bedroom with a cup of hot chocolate and some biscuits we had baked the day before with the girls in the big kitchen. At first I thought it must be a birthday, it seemed so special. But then Eva said, 'Sit down, Puppe. I have something very serious to ask you, and I would like your opinion on it.'

I was thrilled. I was so used to being 'the little one', the one who did what she was told by all the older members of the family, that it felt wonderful to me to be taken into Eva's confidence.

'Do you miss Mutti?' she asked.

'Oh, yes,' I said honestly. 'Very much.' It was true. I had really, really, really missed her, despite how loving Eva was and how welcoming everyone had been at Tabarz.

'You know, don't you, that the war is not going well for us any more and that the Allied soldiers are coming into Germany. It means that life will be difficult and perhaps dangerous. I think we should go back to Wiedersdorf and be with Mutti. Would you like that?'

I nodded. As soon as she said it, I knew that there was nothing I wanted more.

'Do you think you are strong enough to try to get to her? It will mean lots and lots and *lots* of walking.' Eva looked at me seriously.

'Yes, of course,' I said immediately. 'I can do it, I know I can.'

I was so proud that Eva had asked my opinion. I would have followed her to the ends of the earth anyway, but the way she treated me as a grown-up really made sure that I would willingly agree, no matter how daunting the task seemed. I felt very adult and important to have been consulted.

'It is not like the walks we go on with the girls. It will mean a real journey. Wiedersdorf is many miles away and we will be walking for days. Do you think you can manage it?'

'I know I can,' I answered. 'I am very good at

walking.' I had no real idea of what it meant, but I knew that if Eva wanted to go, I wanted to go with her. She would never have left me, so if I had said no we would never have started on our long march.

'Then we will go tomorrow,' said Eva decisively. She smiled at me. 'You are very brave, little one. I know we will get to Mutti safely, I am sure of it. But tonight you must get a good night's sleep. I don't know when or where we will be able to sleep again.'

I did not know whether to be excited or afraid, but I knew I was looking forward to seeing Mutti again. That night, I went to bed and fell asleep talking to Charlotte, telling her all about Mutti and how we would soon be with her.

5

The Journey Begins

The night before we started our odyssey, Eva wrote a quotation from Nietzsche into her diary. It said simply:

Never let the hero in your soul die.

Then she took my small pink blanket and with needle and thread turned it into a miniature rucksack. The next day we packed into it my spare pants, vests, stockings and an extra cardigan. She told me I was only allowed to take Charlotte, nothing else.

I was wearing long trousers and a double-breasted red cardigan with a hood and mother-of-pearl buttons, which Eva had knitted for me. Everyone called me Little Red Riding Hood. My pale leather shoes came up over my ankles, as at that time there was a saying in Germany: 'Children should be taught the importance of looking after their ankles.' Eva was wearing her ski trousers, a blouse and the warm blouson jacket that she also wore for skiing, and brogues on her feet. We both wore headscarves, mine a lovely red and white one that Mutti had given me to match my jacket. It covered my hair, which was in plaits, with a pretty comb holding a roll of hair on top of the head. It was the fashion back then and we called it a *Tolle*.

The girls at the home had made me a small wooden cart with a handle to pull it. This is where my rucksack and Charlotte travelled. We had a torch and we took some provisions: rye bread, which was baked at the home, spread with liver pâté, and some with honey for me. We took two packets of Zwieback, which is a cross between a biscuit and a rusk. Ours were plain, but in better times you could get them coated with chocolate or cinnamon icing.

We took two shallow, thick china dishes, too, which doubled as plates and cups.

Eva had some money that Mutti had given her. She also had her own savings in the Post Office, but I don't think she had time to withdraw any before we left. Sixty years later I cried when I saw in her diary the simple records she kept of her finances. At the top of the page, alongside the Post Office account number, she wrote, 'Important Information: In the event of my death, this money goes to Bärbel.')

We were not alone as we set off. We had the company of four girls who worked at the home. Lo, Hanna, Hilde and another whose name I cannot remember, walked and spent the first night with us. Nature was on our side. We had lovely, warm spring weather and the fruit trees along our route were beginning to blossom, throwing out sprays of white and pale-pink flowers. I can remember the tangy, clean smell of crushed pine needles in the woods, and the springy feeling of the moss and fern beneath my feet, like a carpet. Everywhere we went, we saw daffodils and wild crocuses, and tiny violets at the edges of ponds and rivers. This was not so difficult, I thought. In fact, it was more like fun.

Eva had a compass and a map with her, and she knew the route we should take. We had to head north and west to get to Wiedersdorf, where we last saw Mutti. Our path took us alongside the track of the little train, which was no longer running, until we reached another village in the forest, Friedrichroda.

As we approached the village, a dull, droning sound in the distance quickly developed into a roar. Suddenly, a plane thundered overhead and immediately, with a great throbbing and noise, hundreds of them seemed to be on top of us, flying above the treetops, heading towards the village and strafing everything in their path with bullets.

I heard the rat-a-tatting of bullets as they hit the road and saw the bright flashes of fire light up the planes' wings before Eva grabbed my hand and pulled me into the undergrowth, where we lay, with the other girls huddled nearby, for several terrifying minutes.

Guns barked around us and the shadows of the planes flitted over us. We could hear bullets ricocheting among the houses, then the planes roared away and the anti-aircraft guns fell silent. I stirred, but Eva told me to lie still. My legs and arms were getting stiff and cold, but she made me stay there until she was sure we could go on. We crawled out from under the bushes and without even discussing what we had seen and heard, we carried on walking. Everybody else in the village was still taking cover and we were the only ones on the deserted road.

It was our first introduction to the perils of the journey.

By nightfall, as the warmth of the day disappeared and the cold darkness fell, we had reached the village of Finsterbergen, without any more attacks. We found our way to the Hotel Linde, which was a hostel similar to the one at Tabarz where we knew we would be welcome as we had been given a letter of introduction from Miss Ramelow, the head of the Tabarz home.

There were soldiers billeted at the hostel. At first I was in awe of them and a little frightened. They seemed big and forbidding in their uniforms, with their heavy boots, which made such a noise when they walked, but they smiled, patted my head and one of them gave me a biscuit, so I forgot my fears. Later, they generously shared their meal with us. It was really good: rice with lots of meat. Meat was scarce and to have such a plateful was wonderful.

We shared a dormitory with the girls who had walked with us, but there were several air raids in the night, which meant we had to go down to the cellars. It must have been difficult for Eva, as I was heavy and drugged with sleep, and wanted to stay in my bed. But she would whisper, 'Wake up, Puppe, darling,' and take me in her arms, shaking me to hurry me into wakefulness. We slept in our clothes, as we would do every night of our long trek.

The next morning, at 7 a.m., we prepared to set off again, first saying goodbye to our four companions who were going to make their way back to Tabarz. All the girls cried as they said their farewells.

'Are you sure, Eva?' asked Hanna. 'Do you really want to go on?'

'Please, come back with us,' pressed Lo, her face worried.

Eva was insistent. 'We have to go on. We've started now. But thank you for coming this far with us. I promise we'll be fine. Look after yourselves as well.'

We all wished each other luck with tearful hugs and kisses, and set off on our way again.

We were on the road towards Georgenthal. Whenever we reached crossroads or junctions where Eva was not sure of the route, she would look at the compass and take the road going north. We had to depart from our planned route several times and when I retrace the route we followed on a map I can see that we walked miles out of our way, always to avoid pockets of fighting. It meant we spent many of our first few days walking to no avail, as we circled and didn't move forward. Luckily for us, the road signs were intact. Later, I read that the Allies were surprised when they reached Germany to find there were road signs; in Britain they had been removed to foil the enemy in the event of invasion.

As we walked in the early morning, our surroundings were lovely. There was an ethereal mist clinging to the ground among the trees, which looked magical to me. The countryside we were walking through was breathtakingly beautiful: today it is a national park. There were gentle hills on the horizon and the hazy grey dawn soon cleared into strong, crisp spring sunshine. Although man created death and destruction, and brought suffering and sorrow to so many ordinary people on both sides of this terrible war, nature was oblivious and celebrated the rebirth of warmth in the earth with her usual profligate beauty.

We held hands and sang songs to keep up our spirits, and because, as Eva rightly pointed out, you walk faster if you are marching to the beat of music. One of the songs we sang was called 'The Hamburger Homeland' song and was obviously written after the bombing of the city:

Where Schulau lies on the beautiful
    River Elbe,
Where all that is left of Hamburg is a
    pile of rubble,
Where there are so many ruins, endless
    heaps of stones and bricks,
That is where my homeland is,
That is where I am at home.

Where the bombers circle at night in the
    sky above us,
Where all around everything is up in flames,
Where the windows shatter and the
    lights go out,

That is where my homeland is,
That is where I am at home.

Where the enemy kills wives and children,
Where there are so many casualties to
    be mourned,
Where tired eyes are full of tears,
That is where my homeland is,
That is where I am at home.

Where so many cries for help can be heard,
Where so many family homes lie in ruins,
Where so many people lost all that
    they owned,
That is my Hamburg, my homeland,
Fought for with German blood.

I can also remember singing a song about the *Luftwaffe*, which went something like 'High in the sky like an eagle, the *Luftwaffe* is at home'. It had a good beat, which really got us moving. All German children, especially those old enough to be in the BDM or the Hitler Youth, learned these patriotic songs, but to us they were just music with a rhythm to march to. Mostly, we sang German folk songs, which I had learned in kindergarten. One of us would start singing, then the other would join in. We'd been taught to harmonise, so we practised as we walked and giggled when it went wrong.

We saw other people on the road, but there was no time to stop and talk or make companions. People scurried along purposefully, everyone trying to reach their own destination and keeping themselves to themselves, perhaps scared of getting too friendly with strangers.

We had not walked more than a mile or two when a military car pulled up alongside us and the two soldiers and driver offered us a lift. We gladly piled in and they took us as far as the Steigerhaus, a local landmark. It was a large house built early in the century for a Prussian princess, but used at this time as a hunting lodge for senior members of the Nazi government. That was where the soldiers were bound for and they dropped us nearby. As we got out, one of them gave me a bag of Printen, special German ginger biscuits covered with chocolate, which we traditionally eat at Christmas. They are delicious and Eva allowed me to eat one straight away. The walk was still a novelty to me and I thought to myself, 'Great! I will get presents all along the way.'

Eva wrote in her diary:

When he handed her the biscuits, little one smiled with her great big eyes.

'You mustn't eat them all at once,' Eva said. 'We must make them last. So we should limit them to one each evening, as a reward for all our hard walking.' In the evening, I always offered the bag to her when I took mine and she would take one. But I know she never ate it. When she thought I was asleep, she would secretly put it back into the bag, so that the supply lasted longer for me. It was a simple act of selfless generosity I have remembered all my life.

Walking on from the Steigerhaus, we came upon an area of heavy fighting. Eva wrote:

There was shooting and banging everywhere, from all sides. The shells were whistling past us. We were very, very scared.

We had stumbled into the pathway of the American assault on Germany. The war was not yet over and there were fierce pockets of fighting all around us but we pressed on, trying to stay out of the way of danger and hopeful that we would find shelter when we reached the village. We were just a mile or two away from Georgenthal when we stopped to rest on a bench under a tree. If there hadn't been the sharp patter of sporadic gunfire and the whine of the grenades, it would have been a lovely spot to rest. It was only April, but the sun was hot enough for us to have taken off our jackets and we were glad of the shade from the tree.

While we were sitting there a middle-aged man dressed in green with a rifle over his shoulder and a pair of binoculars dangling round his neck came towards us.

'Is he a soldier? Is that why he's wearing a uniform?' I whispered to Eva.

'No,' she replied in a low voice. 'He's a forester.'

'Where are you heading?' he called as he approached.

'We're trying to get to Georgenthal,' said Eva.

The forester looked serious at this. 'You'll never

get there. They're fighting everywhere, in the village and on the road. The Americans are advancing in that direction. It's not safe, you will definitely be killed if you go that way. You should head instead for Stutzhaus.'

'Thank you,' said Eva politely and the man vanished as quickly as he had arrived. Then she looked worried. 'I don't know how we'll get to Stutzhaus. I've no idea of the way. Come on, sweetheart, we'd better get moving.'

We stood up but before we could set off again two German soldiers appeared, tin helmets on their heads and rifles in their hands. Their trousers were tucked into their knee-length socks and I noticed that their boots were very muddy.

'Where are you going, ladies?' they asked and, when Eva explained, said, 'We're heading for Stutzhaus too. We can take you with us if you like. We're going cross-country. It will be much safer than following the roads. The American artillery are bombarding them non-stop. Come on.'

Gratefully we went with them. We started off following a track, but very soon we were making our way through woods and even crawling through undergrowth when there were sounds of gunfire. We skirted fields, keeping to the hedgerows and ducking into ditches whenever we heard any sound of engines. It was only the second day of our march, but already I had learned to throw myself into a hedge, a ditch or any indentation in the land whenever the sound of firing was close. We knew that when we heard the whine of a shell, we had to get down.

If there was no cover, Eva told me to lie as flat as I could on the ground and keep still. 'If the enemy see you,' she said, 'they will think that you are already dead.'

The two soldiers knew the way and guided us expertly. They were very patient. I could not travel as fast as they could and must have held them back, but they didn't say anything. As soon as we got close to Stutzhaus they stopped.

One gestured towards the town. 'That's where you're going. Just keep straight on and you'll come into town. OK?'

'Thank you so much,' Eva said, 'we would never have made it without you.'

'You're welcome.' With that they disappeared into the woods.

As we walked towards the town I asked Eva, 'Why were they on their own? Shouldn't they be with other soldiers?'

'They're probably scouts,' she answered. 'Perhaps they were sent out to discover where the Americans are and find out what's going on, and they're on their way back right now to report to their unit. Or they could be messengers, taking news from their unit to headquarters.'

'They are very brave,' I said, wide-eyed.

'They have to do it, Puppe, if they are ordered to. That is what being a soldier is all about. But you're right – they are brave. And probably local men as well.'

'How do you know?'

'Well, they led us right across fields and through forests without any maps.'

In Stutzhaus we went to the village hall to register our arrival, as we would in most of the towns and villages where we spent nights. The Germans are rightly famous for their efficiency, and even as the government was disintegrating and the country was facing defeat, people took pride in handling the problems they faced in an organised manner. Refugees like us would register where we were from and where we were going, and then be given an address where we would be billeted for the night. I don't know whether Eva ever had to pay anything, but I don't think so. Everyone was prepared to help out.

We spent that night in a bakery, which was wonderful because, despite all the windows being blown out, the baker was still making bread. All the smells of my early childhood in Hamburg and the bakery on the ground floor of our apartment block flooded back to me. The scent of proving yeast, the delicious aroma of the newly baked bread, the warmth of the huge bread ovens, the dusting of flour that settled everywhere felt reassuringly comforting and normal in the middle of all the chaos and fighting. More important, we got to eat this wonderful fresh bread, still hot from the bakehouse.

It was another night of little sleep, though. The air raids came throughout the hours of darkness, the shrieking of the alarms sending shivers down my spine when I heard them. Sometimes I was too

would fall down on top of us, then terrifying us as the smell of smoke drifted down to us and we worried we would be burned alive, trapped in the cellar. There was a great deal of shouting and noise as people struggled to put out the fire. We heard later that some of the residents had been killed.

No, the most memorable event was something I would, over the next few days, become familiar with. But the first time is etched deep into my memory, even though I did not actually witness it. Beneath the window of the room where we were attempting to rest, we heard a loud commotion. As the windows were all shattered, it was impossible to avoid the noise outside. There were soldiers in the village and we could hear them shouting questions at someone, demanding his papers. Apparently he did not have any, or they were not the right ones, or he was refusing to co-operate. They shot him. It was a single shot and, although I was already familiar with the sound of firing, I had never heard it so close. And I had never heard a human being shot in this way. Fighting in the distance was impersonal: we did not see or hear the bullets strike their targets. This was different. I had heard a gun fired and a man died at that very instant. To have someone shot dead under our bedroom window was extremely shocking.

Eva was aware of what was happening when the soldiers began interrogating the man and struggled to distract me. She started telling me a fairy story, but both of us could hear clearly the barked questions and the mumbled replies, then the sickening report of the single bullet. Afterwards there was the sound of the soldiers moving on, then silence. Nobody moved the body.

I hope that the next day somebody gave the dead man a decent burial, but I don't know. I have since often wondered who he was and how he came to meet his death in Stutzhaus in the way he did. He may have been an American scout, although we thought he was speaking in German, not English. He may have been a deserter from the German army. He may have been one of the farm labourers who were brought into Germany from the Balkan states and who liberated themselves when the end of the war was in sight. He may also have been an Italian: after Italy pulled out of the Axis in the autumn of 1943 the Italians were the enemies of

Germany and many of them who were in the country were shot. Whoever he was, I felt very sorry for him, and often in later years I have wondered whether his mother and father or brothers and sisters ever knew what happened to him. Was he married? Did he have children growing up who would ask, 'Where is Daddy?' But I also felt great sympathy for the soldiers who had to shoot him. In the confusion and panic of those last days of the war, they thought they were doing what was right. These were abnormal times and terrible things were happening everywhere.

6

Eva Nearly Loses Me

The next day at 6 a.m. we set out again. I remembered clearly what I had heard in the night but as we left the bakery I did not see the body of the shot man. Perhaps it had been moved or, more likely, Eva skirted round the building away from it. As always, she sheltered me as best she could from what was happening around us. She told me to carry Charlotte as we walked along, which I was only too happy to do, and when she said 'Charlotte', it meant I had quickly to put the doll in front of my face and only look down at the ground so that

I could see where my feet were treading. Eva would hold my arm and guide me, saying, 'I don't want you to look right now.' When she said this I knew it was something serious. Eva wanted to prevent me from seeing the dead bodies along the roadside but I did, of course, catch glimpses. I saw soldiers and civilians, women as well as men, and sometimes I smelled the rotting flesh. It is another of the smells that haunts me, not a happy one. For anyone who has ever smelled it, it is unforgettable.

As we carried on walking there were plenty of occasions for Eva to say 'Charlotte'. The heavy fighting around Stutzhaus had taken its human toll and there were dead bodies lining the roads. When we passed through villages where there had obviously been heavy shelling there were more corpses lying on the ground, and among the smouldering ruins and heaps of rubble.

We saw convoys of German military vehicles, moving under direction to some fresh encounter with the enemy, and we caught glimpses of the sad faces of soldiers who were piled into the backs of trucks, being taken to a battle from which they might never return.

Young as I was, even I knew what was happening. I turned to Eva and said, 'Why don't they just go home?'

Eva had tears running down her face. 'They can't, Puppe. They have no choice. Do you remember what I told you about what being a soldier is? It means you have to do your duty. They can't go home. They have to fight.'

We watched the trucks disappear down the road, taking the soldiers to their fate.

By mid morning, we were walking down a long, straight road, heading towards the village of Crawinkel. The Americans had already been in the area for five days. On 4 April, three days before we set out on our walk, they had liberated the forced labour camp near Ohrdruf, one of the Nazi concentration camps. I can say nothing to expiate the guilt of my nation over such horrors, but I can truly attest that we knew nothing about it. I had a child's eye view of the war and was sheltered from as much of it as possible, but my sister and the rest of my family were just as ignorant of the appalling things that were being done to human beings in the camps. As we walked through the area, we did not even know of its existence.

The atmosphere became menacing. We could hear the rumble of heavy artillery, like the constant growl of thunder, then the pitter-patter of small-arms fire. Tracer from the guns tracked across the sky like fiery shooting stars. To our left, the land swept away from the road, a patchwork of open farm fields, punctuated by the distant grey spires of churches in hidden villages, and to the right it rose steeply and was heavily wooded with fir trees. We were the only two people on the road: the place was strangely deserted. The fighting seemed to be far off and then, suddenly and without warning, there were planes overhead, swooping down and strafing the road with bullets. Other planes came and a real dogfight began above the fields to our left. Because the ground fell away, they seemed to be flying at almost the same level as the road and I could clearly see the pilots, and the American and German insignia on the wings.

We were stunned for a moment, and watched the extraordinary sight of the planes darting in and out of combat, stuttering bullets at each other as they flew. Then Eva realised the danger we were in. 'Get down!' she shouted, and we both flung ourselves flat into the small hedge on the left-hand side of the road. We lay there, listening to the explosions, terrified, until the planes roared away. But it was not over: artillery fire was coming from the fields below us and the bombardment was fierce, with shells exploding all about us. We lay still, petrified, in the hedge. Shells must have struck the hedge further along, because it shook violently from time to time. Eva stretched out her hand and found mine, and she told me again not to move. My left leg was in a puddle and my right was growing stiff because I had it at an awkward angle, but I did not dare to shift it. The earth, in the early morning spring sunshine, had been warm at first touch, but a deep cold had seeped through and into my bones. I was so still that ants began to crawl up my cheek and I had to move my head against the earth to dislodge them. Charlotte was in my arms, but we had left our little cart on the road. I squeezed my eyes tight shut and tried to think of nice things, a trick Eva had taught me. I thought of Mutti and our home in Hamburg, and playing at the brick factory, and of my little puppy, Lumpie. I thought of

Breathless and scared, we rested for a few seconds. But the soldier, who was still holding my arm, spoke quickly: 'Come on, there's no time to hang about. We have to get you up the hill.'

He set off, holding me tight to one side and Eva to the other. She carried the cart that contained all our possessions. Together, we made our way up the steep hill. There was no track and we were forcing our way through the undergrowth, going round trees, upwards, always upwards. It seemed to my little legs to go on for ever. I was struggling to breathe and was unbearably tired but we forged on, the noise of the guns roaring above us. The soldier had a strong grip on my hand and was propelling me forward, which helped me to carry on.

But at the top of the hill disaster struck. He let go of my hand for a second, to clear away the brushwood that was in our path. I had been relying on him completely and at the moment he took away his grip I fell back, tumbled and rolled backwards down the hill. It seemed that I was falling for an age, as I rolled and bumped off trees, bounced through the undergrowth and slid down the scree. In reality, it only took a few moments for me to reach the bottom of the hill, where I came to a halt at the edge of the wood, right back where we had started.

I was dazed and hardly knew what had happened. Terrified, bruised and exhausted, I heard someone shouting 'Stay still!' so I lay motionless, obeying the order but also remembering what Eva had told me about pretending to be dead so that the enemy would ignore me. I concentrated on pressing my body as flat as I could on the hard earth. My right leg was twisted under me and pain from it began to throb through my whole body. I was bruised and cut, and in a state of shock.

I heard the whine of shells and the dull thump as they hit the hillside above me, followed sometimes by the groaning of trees uprooted by the explosion. In reply came the angry stutter of gunfire. At the top of the hill, Eva clutched her hand over her mouth to stop herself screaming. I was so still that she was convinced I really was dead.

I seemed to lie there for an eternity, but then I heard the crackling of twigs and a voice close by me saying, 'Come on, run for it.' A large hand took hold of mine and I was pulled to my feet again. It was the same soldier. He had risked his life again to come down the hill for me. He half dragged, half carried me to the shelter of the trees, then paused and grinned at me. 'Right, kid,' he said, 'we've got to get up this hill again, get you safe.'

I felt safe already, from the moment that his rough hand encircled mine. Silently I clutched his fingers again and we made the long climb back up the hill. This time he made sure that he never relaxed his tight grip on me.

We made our way up, through the tangle of undergrowth, following tracks made by deer or other woodland creatures. Near the top, in a clearing, Eva was waiting, crouched down behind a pile of logs. As we approached, she rushed forward and took me in her arms, hugging me tight. Then she started to brush the leaves and twigs from my clothes, and retied my red-and-white headscarf over my fair plaits. 'Oh, Puppe, I thought I had lost you,' she said, sobbing with relief. 'What would I have told Mutti? And how could I go on without you, little one?'

More soldiers came out from the bushes and we were hastily bundled into a safe spot behind some logs. Eva could not stop hugging me and fussing over me. We sat together, our backs to the logs, and clutched each other.

The planes had gone, but the artillery bombardment continued. Eventually the firing abated and we came out of our hiding place. We discovered that we were in a small encampment of soldiers, screened by the trees but with a good vantage point to see across the valley. There were about a dozen, all of them very friendly.

'Hey, what an adventure you've had, kid! That'll be something to remember, won't it?' said one. 'Let's take a look at those bruises and make sure you're all right.'

My cuts and bruises were carefully inspected. I was remarkably undamaged: there is an old saying that little children and drunks know how to fall, and I think it must be true. But I was badly shaken, and they were all anxious to cheer me up and make me relax. 'Come and sit down over here,' they said, 'and we'll get you something to eat.'

They made comfortable places for us to sit and set about making us a meal. It was still early, but they were used to seizing any break they had. It was like a little party. We had white bread and strawberry jam, Eva had tea and I had hot chocolate, made from sachets, which came with the milk and sugar already in them. We even hummed a little song, but not too loudly, so that our hideout would not be discovered. The soldiers joined in, eating and drinking hot drinks, and chatting to us in low whispers. They pulled crumpled, dog-eared photos of their own children from their pockets to show us, and talked wistfully about their homes and their families.

The one who rescued me was the tallest and the best-looking of them all, a very handsome young man, slim with dark hair. For many years afterwards he was my dream hero, my knight in shining armour. When I was teenager I used to fantasise that one day I would meet a man like him, fall in love and live happily ever afterwards. I am sure that I idealised him but to me he was everything you could want in a man: courageous, good-looking and charming. I can't remember his name, but I never forgot his face or what he did for me that day. I wonder what became of him and whether he survived the war. I hope he did.

Eva, too, always treasured the memory of him, because she really was sure for a few minutes that I was dead and was beside herself that it was her fault.

Before long, the soldiers had to move on. Our party, a tiny moment of carefree friendship and happiness, had to come to an end because their camp was no longer safe after the attacks. They took us with them to their vehicles. There was a tank, and some big lorries with machine-guns, and others full of equipment and large canisters of petrol. They lifted us up into a lorry with camouflaged sides and a bench along each side. Eva and I sat there, swaying with the movement of the truck as they drove us towards the next town. One of them gave me a bag of sweets.

'Where shall we drop you?' they asked.

'Can you put us down near Marlingen? I have a letter to hand over there,' said Eva. Someone in Tabarz had given it to her to deliver if she could and here was the opportunity.

'Sure. You girls take care now.'

We said goodbye to our new friends on the outskirts of the village, grateful for all their help. The kind soldiers gave us more bread and a pot of jam to take with us. It had been quite a day and it wasn't over yet.

In her diary Eva wrote:

> You cannot imagine how scared I was, and I cannot describe what I felt when little one rolled all the way down the hill. We had so much good luck.

She also wrote about our delight in getting the bread and jam:

> How our tummies were jumping with joy!

As we walked into Marlingen, Eva was in a good mood. 'That was very lucky,' she said. 'Not only have we had an escort here and saved ourselves some walking, but we should be well looked after and given somewhere nice to sleep.'

But it wasn't like that all. Unlike in most of the towns we went to, our welcome was distinctly chilly and after a short time we were sent on our way. Eva wrote:

> we really had great expectations of being looked after, and having a good night's sleep. But all we were given were potato pancakes, they couldn't have cared less.

Of course, people were all very scared at the end of the war and could be apprehensive of strangers. I love potato pancakes, which are made by grating potato, mixing it with egg and frying it, and then eating it with apple sauce, so I was probably quite happy, but it must have been a let-down for Eva. It is perhaps surprising that the people there were happy to let a young woman and child go walking off alone into the night, but the circumstances were hardly normal. For the most part we experienced great kindness, so we couldn't complain.

As usual, Eva hid her disappointment from me and we walked on. Because we had nowhere else to stay that night, we slept in a ditch. Fortunately the weather was warm and we found a dry place with bushes around to shelter us from any wind. The temperature dropped at night, but we put on our extra jumpers and cuddled up close together. I don't know how well Eva slept, but I was so tired that I went out like a light, before she even had time to comb out my hair and make me say my prayers. Normally, sleeping outdoors would be a great adventure, but I was too exhausted to appreciate it. Instead, huddled close to my big sister in a hedge, I fell into blissful unconsciousness.

7

A Little Music in Our Lives

At daybreak we woke up and got ourselves together. It was the fourth day of our walk and we had not made much progress because the fighting was forcing us out of our way, so we set off early, hoping to press on. Luck was on our side again: a farmer came by on his horse-drawn open cart and offered us a lift. So for six or seven kilometres we sat with our legs dangling over the edge of the cart, savouring the luxury of not having to walk.

When the farmer dropped us off we walked on, throwing ourselves into the ditch or scrambling under the cover of the woods when we heard the sound of planes or fighting. On one occasion I struggled to my feet after a raid and found Eva laughing at me: I had plunged into the grass so hard that my cheeks were stained green. Another time I was upset because I found I had crushed a whole bed of tiny blue forget-me-nots.

There were more people on the roads now, some of them going the same way as us. Although we kept to ourselves, occasionally we would walk with others, especially if they knew the way. Sometimes, near the towns and villages, there were deep trenches called *Panzergraben*, literally 'tank graves', dug by the local people to halt the progress of the American tanks, and we would cower inside these when we heard the sounds of guns. That day there was a particularly heavy attack and we were both very scared. Eva wrote:

> The enemy attacked again, so we went back into the woods. It was quite some attack and we were really not sure we would come out of it alive. I found myself thinking

'Is this it? Is this the end? Will we die here?' Afterwards, we were relieved to have escaped unhurt, but very worried about the future.

I think Eva was beginning to realise just how dangerous our journey was and what a risk we were taking. When we emerged from sheltering in the woods, we saw a knot of soldiers talking to a man who was clearly a foreigner. He was a big man, wearing a dark overcoat. A German officer was challenging him and there was an air of hostility. 'Where are your papers?' the officer shouted, obviously angry. Then he pulled his pistol out of his belt.

Eva moved at once to shield me from seeing but it was too late. I saw the officer aim and fire. I heard the loud report of the gun and saw the man's body crumple and slump down on the ground. He lay still, with a damp patch oozing on his chest. I was shaking from head to toe as Eva took my hand and pulled me quickly onwards. 'Don't think about it, Puppe. Think about nice things,' she said.

We kept walking swiftly along the road, away

from the horrible scene we had just witnessed. She started singing, and after a while I tried to forget what I had seen and joined in. She was not being heartless: I know from talking to her years later that she was as shaken as I was and as distressed. But her mission was to get me through alive and with as little trauma as possible. This was what kept her going.

We realised we were walking through what had been, only minutes earlier, a battlefield. It was a terrible and unforgettable sight. There were the bodies of soldiers all around and field ambulances loading up the wounded. Tanks and army vehicles were dotted about in smoking pyres, some of them still in flames. Men ran about with stretchers collecting the injured, and the air was filled with the groaning sounds of soldiers in pain and occasionally a shrill cry of agony.

Some soldiers were crouching over the bodies of others who were lying so still that they seemed dead.

'What are they doing?' I asked Eva.

'They are checking whether the men are still alive or not. If they're not, they will remove their identity discs. All soldiers wear them on chains round their necks so that they can be identified, and then their relatives can be told what has happened.'

I watched wide-eyed. Please, please, I prayed, please don't let Father be lying somewhere dead, with someone taking his disc to tell us, his family, that his war is over and that he is never coming home.

I wondered then, and I still wonder today, if the soldiers buried their own dead and the enemy's side by side in the same graves. Later in life I learned the German proverb '*Wir betrauern die Toten — doch Sie haben ihren Frieden*'. It means 'We mourn the dead — but they have found their peace'. I say it to myself when I think back on this scene.

We stumbled away from the area of fighting, glad to leave this sorrowful place behind us, and we were joined as we walked by two soldiers. We were very glad to meet them as they knew the way. They introduced themselves as Officer Stern and Mr Osterman.

They took us to Grafinau, a village near Oberihm, where there was an army hospital and they managed to persuade someone at the hospital to give us a room for the night. We were shown into a room with two beds, and the soldiers shared one while Eva and I had the other. We were too tired and too pleased to have a bed after our night in the ditch to care about this, and they were decent young men. They slept with all their clothes on, including their boots, as they said it was important to be ready to run at any time if we had to. I had never slept in a room with strangers before and I thought it was funny, especially as one of them snored. I'd heard my father snore, but that seemed a long time ago.

After sleeping for a short while, I woke up and lay awake listening to the whimpering and the cries of the wounded soldiers in the hospital wards. There was another terrible cocktail of smells to haunt my nostrils for evermore: this time the smell of blood and flesh, poor sanitation and disinfectant. The door to our room was half open, perhaps for the quick exit the soldiers had warned us we might need to make, and the dim light outside in the hall meant that sometimes I would see a nurse or a doctor go by, casting shadows that grew large until they filled the doorway and then receded to nothing. I went to sleep again, after saying a prayer to thank God that we were not injured or in pain.

Although Eva and I were cramped together in a single bed, it was much more comfortable than sleeping in a ditch and we allowed ourselves a lie-in. It was eight o'clock the next day before we moved on, walking to Oberihm. Officer Stern and Mr Osterman continued walking with us and we enjoyed their company. We felt safer with them, although that was probably a false sense of security, as their uniforms were more likely to attract enemy fire than we would on our own. But we believed that the enemy would kill us all anyway, if they found us, so it made no difference.

It was a long day of walking with the usual efforts to avoid the fighting and the overhead attacks, and we were very pleased when at last we saw the town in front of us.

Mr Osterman knew the area well. 'My sister lives in Oberihm,' he said. 'I'm sure she will be able to help you.'

He was right. When we reached the town, he

took us to his sister's house and she was happy to find us accommodation for the night. The house next to where she was living had been bombed, but the wine stored in the cellar had miraculously escaped. A few bottles were given to us. We stayed in the cellar of a large villa, where the family had created a comfortable living area. There were no windows, of course, as it was below ground, but it was remarkably civilised. There were children in the family, although they were already fast asleep in bed when we arrived so I didn't meet them, but I was allowed to play with their toys. There was a small makeshift kitchen with a stove, and there was even a downstairs washroom and toilet, and the towels had yellow ducks embroidered on them. Everyone had blow-up camping mattresses with pillows and blankets. Eva and I pushed our two 'beds' together in a corner, and pulled a curtain round us for more privacy. It was very cosy and I felt safe.

Eva stayed with me until I was asleep. Every night she massaged my legs, especially if we had walked a long way, to relieve the muscles after the long hours of walking. My legs felt very heavy and I struggled to lift them by the end of each day, and I would get terrible pains in my hips. Eva would rub them and comfort me, and she always had a positive explanation for everything. 'They are growing pains,' she would say. 'You are going to be so much taller from all this exercise.'

Despite my fatigue and the pain in my legs, I always felt better after Eva had massaged me. She had the most wonderful way of soothing me and making me feel secure, even in the chaos we were living through. She was my anchor, holding me firm in these rocky seas. After she had rubbed my legs at night, I would offer to rub hers and she would let me. 'That's lovely,' she would say. 'That feels so good.' She always told me how much better she felt afterwards, even though my little hands were just stroking the surface.

Every night, Eva carefully combed out my hair and re-plaited it. She was very worried that I would pick up headlice, so she combed it through hard. It always made me think of Mutti, who had plaited my hair every night at home, and had grumbled at me for being such a tomboy and having so many knots in it. I longed to have Mutti brush my hair again, even if she were to scold me while she was doing it.

After I was asleep that night, Eva and our friendly soldiers stayed up talking and drinking the wine, and she wrote in her diary that it was a pleasant evening.

The next day we were up and, having said farewell to Officer Stern and Mr Osterman, were on the road again at 7.30 a.m., after washing and cleaning our teeth. Although we never changed our clothes for two whole weeks and kept them on even at night, Eva had soap and a towel, and she made sure I washed and cleaned my teeth. If we stayed in houses, we had the use of toilets and bathrooms, but when we were on the road we washed in streams. Of course, on the road we had no toilet paper, but we became expert at spotting big soft leaves that were not prickly and we would pick them as we walked along, so that we had a supply when we needed them.

The walking wasn't too hard, particularly as we had so many enforced rests as we crouched under hedgerows and lay flat on the ground to avoid the air attacks. When I did get tired, Eva's trust in me and the way she treated me like a grown-up kept me going when I might otherwise have stopped.

We still had some of our bottles of wine, which Eva was carrying in her rucksack as they were too weighty for our little handmade cart. She wrote in the diary:

They were so heavy and they hurt my back so much that I thought about leaving them by the wayside. Luckily, just before I abandoned them, a big army truck pulled over and offered us a lift.

Puppe was on the lap of one of the soldiers, I sat between two of them. When I looked at the man on my right, a little shiver went down my spine. He had such a lovely face, and he was so nice to the little one. The care we both were given by them was something we really needed.

I can remember sitting in the truck. The soldiers were doing everything possible to entertain me, making me laugh by telling me funny stories and pulling faces, and asking me all about myself and my family. They asked me my doll's name and when I told them she was Charlotte they formally introduced themselves to her. Looking back, I can see that they were starved of normal family company and all desperately missed their homes. They were so kind to me but, unwittingly, I was helping them as well, bringing a child's laughter and innocence into their lives for a short time, so they made the most of me while they could.

The lorry took us to a village and there we went to a meeting point for refugees, where we would be cared for and allocated beds. Our billet was a large community hall, where there was a big kitchen full of women and soldiers. We quickly made friends with another young woman called Hanna, who was eighteen, and we found three beds together, mattresses lined up against the wall.

'Where are you from and where are you heading?' asked Hanna.

'We're on our way to Wiedersdorf and we've come from Tabarz.' Eva explained our circumstances. 'What about you?'

'I was also sent away to do war work – on the

land. You know, working on a farm. But I told them I had to go home, now that the end of the war is coming. So the farmer and his wife let me go. I'm heading back to my family.'

It was nice to meet someone like us, who was trying to get home.

Before bed we had a meal. Eva wrote:

One of the soldiers made supper for Puppe and me and Hanna. we were looked after very well. Then we shared the last four bottles of wine and everybody drank a toast to peace. Sometimes it is nice to forget about what is going on around us and just not think about what may happen the next day.

An officer who had been on the truck that gave us a lift sat with us and talked about missing his wife and son. He had met her while they were both at school. Now, he wondered if he would ever see her and his little boy again. The boy's name has stuck in my memory for some reason – he was called

Claus Rudiger. I really hope that Claus Rudiger did get to see his father again. The officer's devotion to his family and his love for his wife prompted Eva to write in the diary:

> I wonder if I will ever find somebody I can love as much as he loves his wife. It would be wonderful to love and be loved like that, but it must make the pain of separation very hard to bear . . .

The next day, some of the soldiers in the community centre warned us that we should no longer travel in the daytime. 'It's getting too dangerous,' said one. 'There are civilians killed all the time because they stray into the path of the fighting. There's no telling when or where it's going to happen. If you really have to travel, then you must do it at night when you are less likely to be seen.'

'It's true,' added another. 'The number of people killed on the roads is rising every day.'

Eva listened carefully, then took me to one side. 'Did you hear that, Puppe?' she asked. 'I have a feeling that we need to be cautious. We've already used up a lot of our luck and we don't want to be reckless with the rest. The soldiers know what they are talking about.'

'So does that mean we will be walking in the dark?' I asked.

'Yes — if we have to. It'll be very strange at first but you'll get used to it. The only trouble is we won't be able to travel as far as we could in the day-time. But it's better to take longer and get to Mutti alive and well than it is never to get there at all.'

'Oh, yes,' I said, filled with that same over-whelming longing to see Mutti again. We would do whatever it took to make sure we got back to her.

Not only that, but I was glad to have a respite from walking for a little longer. It meant a few more hours' rest — I could sleep as long as I wanted to in the morning. Then, for a huge bonus, we had a wonderful meal of pasta and meat, cooked for us by the soldiers.

We spent most of the afternoon sheltering in the cellar, listening to the sound of mortars tearing into the buildings around us. Everyone stayed cheerful and, because I was the only child, they made a real fuss of me. They took turns telling me stories, either fairy tales or ones they made up, which often featured a little girl like me. We played 'I Spy with My Little Eye', and a game where somebody said a word and the rest had to think of a song with the word in it — and sing the song, of course.

As we were sheltering down there, we heard the whine of a shell coming right over us, extremely close, then there was the dull thud of it hitting a wall, very near by. For a few seconds there was silence, then the sound of falling bricks and masonry. It was a frightening moment as we all wondered if our building was going to collapse but thankfully it stayed intact. We saw, when we emerged later, that the house immediately next door to our building had been hit. One of the soldiers who had been eating with us at lunchtime had been killed. His comrades retrieved his body and managed to bury him. There was an empty hole in the line of houses along the street, like a mouth with a tooth missing, and we all thanked God that our building, where so many people were sheltering, had not taken the direct hit and that only one person had died.

Before we set off, we had a magical half-hour in

the main hall of the community centre. There was a piano, no doubt used for village shows and concerts in the days before the war. One of the soldiers played it for us, performing a piece of beautiful, haunting classical music.

My favourite piece of classical music is Rachmaninoff's Second Piano Concerto. I am not quite sure if this is true, or if it is something that I have believed for so long that I think it is true, but it could be that it was here, in this village hall, in the dying embers of an appalling war, that I first heard it. Even now, whenever I feel sad I play the CD of it and it makes me feel I am being comforted. It carries me off to a different world, and I can leave all my problems and worries behind.

The whole group of us sat around in silence, dreaming and listening to the gentle tinkle of the piano. Eva and I sat together, her arm round me holding me tight. We were both thinking about the flat in Hamburg, where we had a piano and where our whole extended family held literary and musical evenings, when everyone would read a poem or an excerpt from a book, or sing a song. It all seemed a long long time ago. We couldn't help but wonder if we would ever see our family again, or if we would ever get home.

As evening approached, it was time to be off once more. We collected our things, said goodbye to Hanna, who was going in a different direction, and set out. Our luck was in again, and before we had gone too far, we were offered a lift in another army lorry. They said they could take us quite a long way along the road, so we gratefully climbed aboard. The lorry took back routes and little narrow lanes to avoid the areas where the fighting had been fierce during the day. Even at night, the sky would occasionally light up with red and white flares, and the artillery would boom and a red glow in the distance would mean something was on fire. I snuggled down next to Eva in the dark of the vehicle. The driver would switch off the headlights whenever we were in a village or crossing a main road and we would edge forward slowly in the dark. Finally we reached the village of Neckeroda, which is not far from the city of Teichel.

When we got there, Eva decided we should stay. It was the early hours of the morning, but the refugee station was still manned with volunteers despite the hour and we were again billeted in a village hall, lined with camp beds. I was very tired because I had found it hard to sleep during the day, so after we had a meal, which Eva describes in her diary as a cross between supper and breakfast, I went to bed and fell asleep straight away. I did not need any bedtime story or lullaby. Eva wrote about the rest of the night:

Someone had a bottle of liqueur, Kakaonuss. (It's made from chocolate and nuts and is very sweet, the sort of thing you drink after your dessert.) Everybody had a little. There were no glasses, so we simply passed the bottle round. There were so many people that we only had a sip each, so it had no alcoholic effect on anyone. But it was nice to share something and to savour the sweet taste. It made us all feel very companionable, and for a short time the mood was cheerful and relaxed.

After checking that I was all right, Eva sat up for the rest of the night, chatting and flirting with one of the soldiers. His name was Hans and he was a good-looking young man, probably about the same age as Eva, tall and slim with fair hair. He was not married and he and Eva got on really well, but they did not exchange addresses because they both felt that was futile in the situation we were all in. Who could know what would happen to any of us the next day, let alone weeks from now? Besides, we had no address: we were literally homeless and it was very possible that he was, too. If he came from one of the big cities that had been bombed, his family might well have been in the same state as ours. But he gave her a talisman, a keepsake: his watch. It wasn't a valuable watch, but it was all he had that was personal and his to give away. Eva treasured it and when she died, many years later, it was still in her jewellery box.

She wrote in her diary that night:

Thank God sometimes there is a nice hour between all the horrible things that are happening around us. It gives me the optimism and stamina to go on. I hope one day I will find someone I can belong to all my life, because I don't think there could be anything nicer than belonging to someone.

We parted from the soldiers the next day. They went off in a different direction to try to find their unit. Eva never knew if Hans made it through the next few terrible days. I hope he did. He helped my sister so much by flirting with her and reminding her that in the middle of all the horror she was still a pretty young girl. It gave her a desperately needed respite and probably did the same for him. They were just two young people sharing a little romance in the most awful of circumstances. They helped each other get through another night. In wartime, that's all you can hope for. You cannot ask for more.

8

The Witch

We had now been on the road for just over a week. Although we had decided to travel by night, Eva felt we had not made enough headway so the following day, after a really good, late sleep for me, we set off walking in the afternoon towards the village of Orlamünde. We seemed to make slow progress, only travelling a few miles, but several times we had to throw ourselves to the ground because of the sound of grenades and gunfire.

Then, as we walked along, Eva suddenly grabbed my arm and said, 'Listen!'

I strained to hear the sound of more fighting, distant guns, but instead, in the stillness, I heard the call of a cuckoo, a two-note announcement of spring and better times.

'There,' said Eva, grinning at me. 'That will bring us luck. You see, Puppe? Things are definitely getting better.'

We went on, our hearts a little lighter at this good omen.

At Orlamünde we went to the village hall to register and were given an address of a house where we could stay for the night. It was a short way out of the village and we walked there, trundling our little cart behind us, tired and dirty, and looking forward to some food and a night's rest.

As we approached the house, I saw that it looked like something out of a children's story book. I was very happy to see the white-painted single-storey cottage, with its dainty picket fence and fruit trees in blossom in the garden. It was pretty and neat, with snowy white lace curtains, and it seemed to come from a different time before the war, when things were normal and life was peaceful.

As we walked up the road towards it, a woman came out of the front door and waited for us at the gate. She was middle-aged, with her grey hair scraped back into a tight bun, tall, thin and well dressed in a tweed skirt and jacket. To me she looked like a schoolteacher and I felt disappointed; in my imagination the owner of that perfect little house would be small and round and smiley. This woman looked hard and austere. There was a small dog with her, yapping in an agitated way.

Eva and I shared a great love of all animals and we loved dogs in particular, but we were both instinctively very nervous of this one. If it is possible for a dog to have a nasty look on its face, this one did.

The woman came out of the gate to meet us. She gave us both a hug, and stroked my hair and kissed the top of my head. We are a family who are always very demonstratively affectionate with each other, but we were not used to being hugged by strangers. This was sixty years ago, and the kissing and hugging culture we have today did not exist then; we were all rather more formal. So I froze in her clutches, unsure what to do when being embraced by someone I had never met before, or even spoken to.

When she released me she said, 'At last. I've been expecting you.' Eva shot me a look. How could she have been expecting us? Perhaps the telephone still worked locally, or maybe she simply meant she had been expecting someone to be billeted with her, not specifically the two of us. I thought she not only looked like a schoolteacher, but talked like one too. She spoke very well, enunciating each word very carefully, as if she were addressing wayward and slightly dim children.

She took us into the house and my fears were allayed by the fragrant smell of something cooking. We were desperately hungry, not having had anything to eat all that day apart from my biscuits. Our provisions ran out quickly and we were always hungry from our long hours of walking.

Our hostess talked away to us, and all the time she was speaking the dog, which was a mongrel with long hair and about the size of a Jack Russell, was jumping up at our legs and yapping. I bent over to stroke it but it snapped at me and the woman told me to leave it alone. If only it had been willing to leave me alone!

We were taken into a dining room where the table was beautifully set. The woman turned to me and said peremptorily, 'You must wash your hands before you eat.'

I was upset by the way she spoke to me. I had been brought up to wash my hands before eating and although it had not always been possible when we were on the road, whenever I had the opportunity I would wash them, even if it was a matter of rinsing them in a stream. Eva and I both washed our hands and sat down to eat.

The woman poured water for us from a crystal carafe. There was rye bread and butter on the table.

Where was the food? I wondered, still able to smell something delicious and hot somewhere. My poor stomach was desperate for it and I could hardly think about anything else.

But first our hostess wanted to talk to us. Once we had sat down, she cross-examined us about where we were going and where we had come from. Eva politely explained our situation. 'We're heading towards Halle,' she said.

'We're going to our mother,' I piped up.

'Humph!' the woman snorted. 'That's ridiculous.' She turned to Eva. 'Don't you think you are being very irresponsible, taking this young child on a terrible journey like this? You could both end up dead. How would your mother feel about that?'

She harangued us for a few minutes, before at last going out to the kitchen to bring in our food. To my delight, she gave us large platefuls of chicken stew, which we fell upon voraciously. As we ate, she kept up the barrage, hectoring Eva on how reckless she was being. At last she said to Eva, 'You really are not being sensible about this. The best thing you could do would be to leave your little sister here with me. I have plenty of room and I will take good care of her. I have good supplies of food. Then you can go on to find your mother, and when this dreadful war is over you can come back and collect your sister.'

Eva stopped eating and put down her fork. 'That is not possible, I'm afraid, madam,' she said very politely. 'I'm afraid our mother would be very upset indeed if we were to split up or separate. Bärbel and I must stay together. But thank you for your kind offer and for this lovely food.'

As she spoke, her face became very pale. Then she excused herself and went to the bathroom, where she was violently sick.

The woman was unrelenting when Eva returned. 'See, you are not very well. How can you look after a child? You are simply not behaving like an adult about this. Your main responsibility is to Bärbel and you would be doing the best thing possible for her by leaving her here. If I were looking after a child, I would look after her properly, not the way you are looking after Bärbel.'

Eva was looking wretched, so I spoke up: 'I don't want to stay here. I want to stay with Eva and go to find our Mutti.'

The woman looked at me, her face softer than it was when she spoke to Eva. 'Child, what do you know about it? It's a dangerous world out there. And besides, if you stay here in the warm, with good food, you will be fit and healthy when you rejoin your mother.'

I shook my head miserably.

Eva said firmly, 'We're staying together and that's final.'

All the time the little dog was circling the table,

yapping every so often and licking my legs. I tried to push him away, but he always came back. His mistress occasionally fed him titbits off her plate, but he seemed to be more interested in harassing Eva and me. The rest of the meal passed in an uncomfortable silence. She gave us cheese, which normally we would have eaten with relish, but Eva was still feeling very sick and I had begun to feel that I was not well, either.

After we had finished eating Eva said, 'If you don't think we are very rude, we would like to go to bed now. We have another long day ahead of us tomorrow.'

Hardly deigning to speak to us, the woman signalled that we should follow her. She paused at a cupboard in the hallway and took out a large white chamber pot, then led us along the corridor to our bedroom. It was a cheerful, well-furnished little room with two single beds. It should have been the most welcome sight we could imagine, offering us the chance of the best night's sleep we had had for some time. But the little dog got into the room before we did and jumped on the beds without his mistress making any effort to check him. I think he was jealous of our intrusion into his world.

At the doorway the woman handed us the chamber pot. Eva took it without question, but neither of us could understand why we needed it in a house that had a bathroom.

As we were going into the room, towing our little cart behind us, the woman put her arm across the doorway to stop us.

'You can't take that into the bedroom,' she told us. 'You have to leave it in the hallway.'

We had to obey her, so reluctantly we took everything out of it, including my rucksack and Charlotte, and went into the bedroom. The woman called the dog and he trotted out of the room after her.

It was when she shut the door that we panicked. We heard a key turning in the lock from the other side and the sound of her footsteps going away down the corridor. Eva sprang across to the door and rattled the handle, but it didn't budge. We were locked in. It was a shock. Why on earth would she want to lock us up?

'Perhaps she thinks we will steal her precious things,' I said.

'You're the precious thing and she's the one who wants to steal you,' said Eva. As she spoke, she clasped the chamber pot and was violently sick into it.

'Good job she gave us this,' she said as cheerfully as she could. She was pale and I was worried about her. Although I felt sick myself, I think it was caused by the worry. Eva, we decided in a whispered conversation, had food poisoning – and we were pretty sure 'the Witch', as we dubbed her, had deliberately administered the poison. We felt certain she was trying to get rid of Eva, perhaps by killing her or making her so ill that we could not carry on with our journey, so that she could keep me.

The Witch had told us nothing about herself and we hadn't seen a single photograph in any of the rooms we'd been in.

'Perhaps she has lost a child and wants you as a replacement,' suggested Eva.

'Or she might be lonely,' I added. 'Maybe she wants to keep us for company.'

But there was always the possibility that she was simply evil. I had heard the story of Hansel and Gretel, and seen the pictures of the witch in the story books, and all this woman needed was a walking stick, a slightly bent back and a black cat instead of that horrible little dog, and she was the perfect *Hexe* or witch. And she had locked us in, just as Hansel and Gretel were locked up.

We lay down on top of the beds, not taking off our clothes, Eva with the chamber pot next to her so that she could be sick when she needed. I felt more terrified than I had done up to this point in our whole journey: this middle-aged harridan was more frightening to me than any enemy bombardment. I would have lived through another ten dog-fights like the one at Crawinkel rather than face her again. I was literally shaking. I was desperately worried that she really had poisoned Eva and that she would not recover.

All the time we lay there the dog was scratching and whimpering at our door. Occasionally we would hear our hostess shout a command at him, telling him to be quiet, but he took no notice. Her voice just seemed to agitate him and make him scrabble more furiously.

After half an hour or so Eva had stopped vomiting and was feeling a little bit better. Despite being very tired, I had not slept at all because I was so worried about my sister. But I should never have doubted Eva's strength and her determination to keep me safe. When she felt slightly recovered, she got off the bed and tiptoed to the window. She tried to open it and miraculously it slid noiselessly ajar. 'We're not staying here,' she whispered to me. 'She's going to steal you from me. I couldn't bear that.'

We hugged each other tight, grateful for the noise that the dog was making to cover our whispers, as we had no idea whether we were close to the Witch's bedroom.

As quietly as possible, Eva moved a chair across to the window, climbed up and leaned out, gently lowering our rucksacks on to the ground outside. Thank goodness the little house had no upstairs. She gestured to me to come across. Taking Charlotte from me, she dropped her out of the window and helped me scrabble from the chair on to the window ledge. Eva jumped out first: it wasn't far. Then she lifted her arms and I fell into them and was gently lowered to the ground.

It was a great relief to be out of our prison. Eva picked up the rucksacks and I scooped up Charlotte and, holding hands, we began to walk as quietly as possible round the side of the house, looking for the gate in the fence. We had only taken a few steps when, to our horror, we heard the little dog start to bark furiously. Eva grabbed my arm and we both began to run. We could tell from the noise the dog was making that he was no longer inside the house but in the garden. We wondered many times afterwards how he got out. Did the Witch hear us and deliberately set him on us? Did she leave a door open for him all night anyway? Did he have a dog flap that allowed him to get in and out?

However he did it, he came charging round the side of the house towards us. We reached the gate in the picket fence and quickly let ourselves out. Eva paused to close it behind us, hoping it would keep the dog at bay.

We carried on running, leaving the lane to cut across a field. Glancing back, I was dismayed to see that the dog had only been temporarily halted by the gate. Either he had scrambled across it or someone had let him out, but he was in full pursuit again. I had not known that my legs could run so fast. All I could see in my mind's eye was the face

'We have to find somewhere to sleep. You're too tired to go any further, Puppe,' Eva said. She was tired too, especially after her debilitating sickness, but she was feeling much better. 'Nothing that a good run across a few fields couldn't cure,' she said, as ever trying to make light of our problems.

We had thought we would have a cosy night after a good supper, setting us up for our journey tomorrow. But now we were out in the cold darkness, exhausted and without food. Poor Eva didn't even have the good of the meal she had eaten, having thrown it up. We had lost our little cart as well, as we'd had to leave it behind in the hallway of the Witch's house. Things looked bleak, but we pressed on.

After walking a while across more fields, we spotted a farm with some outbuildings. Very quietly, we headed towards a barn, not wanting to disturb any more guard dogs. Eva gingerly pushed open the door to reveal a dry interior with a pile of hay in one corner. Gratefully, we crawled on to it and fell asleep.

9

The Mine

I slept for only a little while before I was woken by a persistent scuffling noise that seemed to be all around us. In the darkness I became aware that Eva was also awake and I could feel the tension in her body.

'It's all right,' she whispered. 'Go back to sleep.'

I could hear the sound of shuffling feet and an occasional low-pitched groaning. There was also a pitter-patter rattling noise that never seemed to stop for more than a second. 'What is it?' I whispered.

'There are animals in the barn. I think there are

a couple of cows and maybe a goat. Don't worry, Puppe. They are farm animals, perfectly friendly.'

'But what is the scratching noise?'

'That's just the sound of them snoring. They don't snore like humans you know.'

It definitely did not sound like the snoring of the two soldiers the other night. But if Eva said it was animals snoring I believed her. I was reassured and was soon back in a deep sleep. Eva must have fallen asleep as well, because the next thing that either of us knew was waking to the sound of a sharp cry.

We opened our eyes to find a woman standing over us with a look of great surprise on her face. We had intended to wake early and be on our way before anyone knew we had been there but, of course, farming folk are up at dawn themselves. The woman, who was small and round and probably in her late fifties or sixties, had come to milk the two cows and the goat.

Eva hastily apologised for our trespass into the barn. 'We are on our way home to our mother and got lost from the main road,' she explained. 'As you can see, I have the little one with me and she could go no further, so we came in here to sleep. We meant no harm.'

The woman said nothing and her expression did not change.

Eva added, 'We can pay you for letting us sleep here.'

'Don't be silly,' the woman said at last and her face cracked into a big smile. 'Just wait here till I milk the animals and then we'll get you inside for breakfast. Here, you can give me a hand.'

I held the full pails to prevent the cows from kicking them over, luxuriating in the warm sweet smell of fresh milk, then Eva and the lady carried them across to the kitchen. She was glad of the help, because it would have taken her two trips to carry it all herself.

As we went, she apologised for being so suspicious of us at first. 'You can't be too careful, in these times,' she said. 'Even of children, I'm sad to say. We've seen plenty of people go through and most cause no harm. But there are always exceptions.'

When we got into the warm kitchen, the farmer was there. He was older and greyer than his wife, and also surprised to see two foundlings appear from nowhere. He welcomed us readily and sat us down at the table. The kindly couple made us a wonderful breakfast of home-baked bread, butter from their cows, plum jam, honey from their own hives and boiled eggs. The farmer's wife poured the fresh milk from the pail through a strainer and offered us each a glass. I can still remember the taste of it. It was warm and sweet, but I could see it in my mind, coming out of the cows' udders in the stable. The thought put me off and I really did not want to drink it; but, not wanting to seem ungrateful, I said it was nice.

The farmer said, 'Give her some more. She won't get good nourishing milk like this very often.'

I smiled, but shot a desperate look at Eva, who understood. Later, when the couple had gone out to feed the chickens, ducks, geese and pigs, she drank it for me. Before we left, we were given a glass of home-made apple juice, which I liked much more than the milk.

When Eva was in the bathroom getting washed, I sat at the kitchen table with the farmer. 'I didn't know cows and goats snored like that,' I said, making polite conversation with our host.

'Like what?' said the farmer, looking surprised.

'Like a rattling noise, like lots of little feet marching.'

He looked blank for a second or two, then laughed. 'Your sister told you that noise was the animals snoring, I bet?'

Eva walked back into the room at this point and the farmer gave her a broad wink. 'She's a good girl, your sister. She's taking good care of you.' He laughed loudly and repeated the word 'snoring' a couple of times. Eva laughed and I joined in, because I knew something had amused them, although I had no idea what.

It was only later, when the walk was long over, that Eva confessed to me. The 'snoring' I had heard had actually been the sound of rats scrabbling around the barn. She had seen two of them, and she had not slept a wink until the sun came up and they scuttled back to their nests. She had been terrified that they would crawl over us if she slept. As usual, she had shielded me from her fears and made sure that I had several hours of sleep.

We lingered over our breakfast, because the farmer's wife was keen to show us photographs of her two sons, neither of whom she had heard from for many months. That could mean they had been sent to the Russian Front, because the Americans and British obeyed the Red Cross rules and sent the German army notifications of any prisoners they took alive, or dead they found. The Russians refused to pass on any information to their enemies. The old couple were clinging to the hope that they were alive in a Russian camp, not dead in unmarked graves. The farmer's wife had tears in her eyes as she showed us certificates her sons had won when they were at school and agricultural college, and the old man said that soon they wouldn't be able to run the farm without help, but they wanted to keep it going in case one or both of their boys returned.

The farmer and his wife filled our rucksacks with bread and strong home-made cheese. Then they pointed us in the right direction and we set off again. Without our little cart I had to carry my own ruck-sack some of the time, but whenever she could, Eva carried it for me. It was a very warm day and we managed to find a clear stream to drink from at lunchtime, before settling down to eat our cheese and bread. For a few blissful moments we lay in the sun, our stomachs full and our legs rested.

In her rucksack Eva carried a small pot of cream, similar to Nivea cream. Every night, before we went to sleep, she rubbed some on my lips and on hers. During the day, when we were very thirsty and there was no sign of anywhere to drink, she would take out the pot and say, 'A little bit of cream will help.' It did, because it moisturised my cracked lips. It also helped psychologically: I always felt better when Eva had put cream on me and to this day I keep a lip salve within reach at all times.

We could hear the rumble of artillery fire in the distance, but we were only forced to lie flat on the ground a couple of times in the whole day, when planes flew over. We had been walking for almost ten days; it was now halfway through April and the countryside was blooming. The land was still heavily wooded on the hillsides, but there were fields of crops in the valley, well tended and looking for all the world as though life were perfectly normal. It was only the background growl of the guns that never allowed us to forget the danger we were in.

Eva used days like this, when we walked for many miles on our own, to teach me. They were never formal sessions, but she would encourage me to learn the names of all the trees and identify their leaves. Years later, when I was in high school, my biology teacher, Mrs Muchow, told the class, 'Bärbel should become a botanist: she knows more about trees and plants than I do.' As we walked along, Eva also taught me my times tables, and she tested me with adding and subtracting, and spelling. She told me stories from history and I remember how one night when we saw a very clear moon, she explained to me that the moon influences the tides.

Towards the evening, we seemed to be walking towards fighting again as we could hear the sounds of fierce conflict, but we saw nothing. The road took us over heavily wooded hills and dropped down into the town of Rudolstadt, which is an ancient medieval city with a castle that dominates the skyline, around which the old buildings seem to huddle. Eva had told me there was a castle and I'd imagined something with turrets and towers, like in a fairy tale, or with a castellated battlement, like the old British castles. So I was disappointed that it was simply a huge palace, built in the eighteenth century on the site of a much older building.

As we walked into the town across the bridge spanning the wide River Saale, the streets were deserted, apart from the odd person scurrying about their business. There was no sign of any soldiers. We asked the way to the town hall and were directed to a red-and-white brick building where a few other travellers were waiting to be allocated rooms for the night. After registering, Eva and I were sent to stay with a family in the town. They were very welcoming to the two tired, dirty strangers and we looked forward to a night of sorely needed rest. Poor Eva was in worse shape than me, after her wakeful night in the rat-infested barn, and was clearly exhausted.

But, as if we had to pay for the beautiful, fairly peaceful day we had spent on the road, that night the bombardment of Rudolstadt started in earnest.

'The American forces are very close,' our hosts told us. 'But we have the cellar we can shelter in.'

Despite our longing for a soft bed and a deep sleep, we had to spend the entire night down in the cellar, as the attack was so ferocious, and there was no let-up. There were other families down there and we all huddled together. A sofa and some makeshift beds were all we had to sit on. I don't know if I slept at all, cuddled up closely against Eva, although I suppose I must have dozed at times. I just remember that the night seemed to last for ever. Even so, it was good to be off the road and to rest our tired legs.

One bright point was that in the corner there was a table with a huge china washbasin, beautifully painted with big roses, and a matching jug that was so big I could never have lifted it. One of the locals brought some boiling water, mixed it with cold from the jug, and Eva and I had a wonderful wash.

The sound of breaking glass told us that the windows of the house above us had been blown out, then there was a huge explosion, which must have shaken the whole town.

'That's the bridge gone,' said one of the men and he was right. The bridge we had crossed only hours earlier had been blown up to halt the American advance. It worked, if only temporarily, because we fully expected to see the streets full of American troops when we emerged from the cellar in the morning, but there was nobody about. The family we were staying with begged us not to try to move on, but we were determined. Eva, of course, made the decisions, but throughout our walk she always consulted me. I was far too young to offer any advice or opinion, but I loved the way she treated me as a grown-up. I agreed with whatever her suggestions were. However tired I was, Eva could always get an extra mile out of me.

Besides, this family had their own problems. As we emerged from the cellar we saw that their house had been damaged. The windows had been blown in, even the frames, and were now ragged holes in the brickwork. There was glass everywhere, some of it propelled with such force that it was sticking into the opposite walls. Torn blackout blinds flapped sadly over the window holes and chunks of plaster had fallen from the ceiling, coating the furniture with a thick white layer of dust.

The house across the street was on fire and still burning. Flames curled out from the naked rafters and, on this windless day, smoke drove straight upwards, as fire fighters struggled to control the blaze. There was a strong smell of blistered wood.

We could not help and we did not want to hinder, so we started out again, heading north-west up the road towards Kahla. The carnage was the worst we saw on the whole journey. There were dead bodies everywhere, not even moved to the sides of the roads. Some of them had been there for a long time, and the stench of decomposing flesh was so great that we took our headscarves off our heads and tied them over our noses.

'Don't look, Puppe,' said Eva sternly. 'I mean it, you must not look. If you do glimpse something, or happen to catch sight of one of these poor things, I want you to look at their feet only. Do you understand?'

I nodded. I didn't want to look and I tried my best not to, but there were so many bodies around me that it was difficult to walk without watching where my feet were going and that meant I could not help seeing the rotting corpses.

But I did as I was told. I looked only at their feet. I can remember to this day the feet of a woman who had lost one of her shoes. Her flesh had turned blue. I caught a glimpse of her skirt, deep purple in colour, almost the same colour as her foot, and I am reminded of her whenever I see the colour. There were bits of mangled carts, horseflesh, twisted metal, fallen masonry and masses of other detritus from the shelling.

We threaded our way through debris from the collapsed buildings until we were out of the town. The corpses still littered the way and we actually saw foxes and big birds, crows probably, scavenging on them. The sound of grenades exploding and heavy gunfire was very close to us. Flares lit up the sky beyond the treetops and there were long, pan-icky bursts of machine-gun fire. We could hear the whistle of shells and the crump of them landing only a few hundred yards away, where we could see plumes of smoke and dust. Occasionally a plane screamed over.

'Let's leave the road,' said Eva. If she was scared, she tried very hard not to show it. 'I think we will be better off if we walk through the woods.'

'What about the path? How will we find our way?' I asked anxiously.

Eva took out her compass. 'Simple. We can use this to guide us. You'll see. Follow me.'

Eva carefully read the compass and used it to lead me through the thick beech wood, following tracks probably made by deer, while all around the trees shook as shells and mortars whined overhead. Occasionally there would be a respite, a small island of quiet, when the noises of the forest would be heard again. Twigs would snap under our feet and birds would flap wildly up into the air, screeching a warning that humans were approaching. How strange that they should be afraid of us, unintentional and harmless intruders into their terrain, when all around was the malevolence of war.

We struggled on for what must have been a couple of hours, because when we emerged from the wood the sun was shining strongly. Here we found a huddle of people taking shelter from the constant firing along the line of trees that marked the edge of the wood. Only a few hundred yards ahead of us German soldiers were gesticulating to us all to come over. We ran across to them and found they were standing by the entry to a mine, which led straight into the side of a hill. Thuringia, the region we were walking through, has many networks of mines beneath its beautiful surface. Coal

work there now. Once we were inside, the darkness was very strange after the bright sunlight outside and we stumbled along a level shaft for a short way until we emerged into a bigger chamber, which was lit by a few petroleum lanterns and the occasional flash of a torch beam.

My eyes adjusted to the new, dim light and I realised that the cavern was full of people, literally hundreds of them herded in together. As we came through, some of them were shouting, 'No more room, no more room!'

They were right – there was barely any room. There were benches along the walls, but they were all filled and the whole place was crammed with people of all ages, from the very old to the very young. One woman was struggling to breastfeed a baby that cannot have been more than a few days old. Toddlers clung to their mothers' skirts, older children cried. Everyone looked totally worn out and wretched. Some people were praying, nervously passing their rosary beads through their fingers.

An elderly man who was sitting on the bench near where we were standing suddenly slumped forward. Nobody took any notice and nobody helped him. Perhaps he had died but it seemed that no one cared at all. Everyone was consumed by their own fear. What would happen to us? Would the Americans come and get us? Would we be blown up, or shot?

Some of these people had been underground for hours: there was a thick stench of sweat. In those difficult days it was hard to keep clean and many of these people seemed to have given up trying. There was no sanitation at all and no food or water. When anyone needed to relieve themselves, they walked a short way down one of the tunnels leading from the chamber. But these tunnels were also full of people, for quite a few yards away from the main area, so they had to push further on to empty their bladders and bowels, and some of them could not be bothered, or were too afraid to go far. This increased the sour stench. I was aware that the ground under my feet was wet and I did not like to think what with. We could not even sit down.

Eva pulled me tight against her, but I could see that she was very frightened. There was a desperate, panicky look in her eyes. Neither of us liked enclosed spaces and this was our idea of hell. (Even today I am terribly claustrophobic – I'd rather swim the channel than use the Eurotunnel. And I cannot bear being plunged into enclosed darkness, which perhaps dates back to this experience.) The noise from people talking, not particularly loudly, reverberated and echoed around the chamber, which was thankfully high, the tunnel having been dug straight into the hillside.

'Come on,' said Eva. 'I'd rather take our chance with the guns than die in here.' She told me later she was seriously afraid that there was not enough air to sustain life for so many people for very long. She started to push our way back towards the entrance, to the annoyance of other people.

'Where d'you think you're going?' a large woman asked her.

'We're going out. My sister is claustrophobic. We'd rather risk it outside.'

'They won't let you,' the woman replied. 'They're guarding the entrance and threatening to shoot anyone who tries to leave. You're not the first one to try to get out, believe me.'

'They don't want anyone giving away that we're here,' a man standing nearby added.

'How long will they keep us here?'

'Probably until the war is over,' said the man. 'Which won't be very long.' He gave a wry laugh.

Eva bit her lip and hugged me even closer. We turned round and pushed back deeper into the chamber, until we found a place where we could sit down. We were near the mouth of one of the tunnels that led away from the main chamber and we sat there for what seemed like hours, watching the strange shadows thrown by the guttering lanterns.

Eventually Eva whispered to me, 'Say that you are going for a wee-wee, then go and explore this tunnel. There may be another way out of here, without guards. You must be very careful, understand? Most important, don't wander off down any side tunnels or you could get lost for ever. Come back in a few minutes, though, no matter what. And do you understand about the side tunnels? Don't go down them. It is very easy to get lost, even if you think you know the route.'

I understood what she wanted me to do.

'I need a wee-wee,' I announced loudly.

'OK,' said Eva, in a voice that could be heard by others. 'Take the torch and go up this passageway until you are nice and private. Don't turn off into any other tunnels.'

She pulled the torch out of her rucksack and gave it to me. We had used it very sparingly up to this point, always aware that the batteries would not last for ever. Even when we had walked at night, we had not used it except to shine briefly on sign-posts.

I stumbled along the tunnel, clear of all the people. I seemed to walk quite a long way and there were often tunnels branching away, but I followed Eva's instructions and stuck to the one I was in. Eventually I came to a small tunnel on my left and at the end of it I could see what looked like day-light. I was worried about going towards it, because of what Eva had told me. So I took my hankie out of my pocket and left it at the junction with the tunnel that would lead me back to her, then I explored the other one and, just as I thought, there was daylight at the end of it. It came from a hole fringed with grass. I put my head through it and there was nobody around, no sign of any soldiers or of the main entrance to the mine, just fields and fields.

I raced back to Eva, remembering to walk slowly when I got near the mouth of the tunnel where the people were. She was waiting anxiously for me – she told me later that she was very worried that she had done a foolish thing letting me go off on my own, in case I had managed to get lost.

I sat down next to her. 'I've found a way out, in a tunnel further up. There's a hole that leads into fields,' I whispered to her.

'Well done, darling. Now, don't let anyone notice what we're doing. We'll be out of here in no time.'

So we behaved nonchalantly, quietly gathering up our things and slipping away up the tunnel together when nobody was taking any notice. We soon reached the hole through which the daylight streamed. I was able to wriggle through quite easily. It wasn't high up, more or less level with my waist. I had to clear some bracken growing across it, but it wasn't hard to get through. Eva passed the two rucksacks and Charlotte through to me. But when she tried to get through, the hole was too small to take her shoulders. She wriggled back inside, then we both started frantically gouging out the earth around the mouth of the hole. We had no tools, so

our fair hair dark and both our faces were covered with smudges of dirt. We stood up, shook as much of the loose dirt off our clothes as possible, and set off walking, cautiously edging round the hill to avoid the entrance where the soldiers stood guard.

At the bottom of the hill we found ourselves in a valley and along it ran a clear stream. We followed its bank until we were sure we were a long way from the mine, then we stopped to wash. From her rucksack Eva produced her beautifully scented soap, given to her by my mother. Both my mother and grandmother loved good-quality soap and they kept it for a long time before using it. They believed that the harder it was, the longer it would last. This tablet did very well: it took us through our whole journey. It smelled of lavender, which is another of the smells that instantly triggers memories of our long trek.

I knelt on the bank and dipped my head in the water, so that Eva could wash my hair, rubbing the soap on to my scalp and lathering it through my curly mop. Then I had to dunk my head again to rinse it. Eva struggled to do the same to her own shoulder-length fair hair and I helped by rubbing up the lather for her. The water was icy cold, but we were both so happy to wash off the dirt that we didn't mind. The sun was strong and warmed us after the shock of the water. We washed our hands and feet, then dried ourselves on the small towel that Eva also carried in her rucksack. We had no food, but Eva had two sweets left, which she said she had saved for a special occasion and this was it. We sucked them slowly, trying to make them last. Then we drank some of the stream water and for a few minutes afterwards we lay resting in the sunshine, with the towel spread out to dry. We were lying in a patch of tall, delicate white flowers; Queen Anne's lace I heard it called years later in England. I looked up at the sky through the froth of tiny blossoms, and it felt as if they were hiding us. My Omi always wore little white lace collars pinned with a brooch, and the flowers made me think of her, with a sharp stab of longing to be at home with my family.

We could not linger, though, no matter how great our relief, so after a short time we carried on. Eva had both the rucksacks on her back and I had Charlotte. Between us, we held the towel, stretching it out to finish drying it, and on we marched.

10

Into the Path of the Invaders

Before long we had rejoined the road and Eva used
the compass to make sure that we were still travelling north-west towards Kirchhasel, which was
the way we wanted to go.

It was eerily quiet. There were no people or
houses and the road was completely deserted. All
we could see were fields stretching to the wooded
horizon and fruit trees lining the side of the road.
We were very scared. We knew, from what we had
heard in the mine, that the Americans would soon
be upon us.

'What will the Americans do to us?' I asked Eva.

She looked very worried. 'I don't know, Puppe. But you know what they have said about the enemies. If it comes to the worst, we may be shot or we may be taken prisoner. Whatever happens, we must be very brave.'

We had been told to fear the Russians more than anything, but we were indoctrinated to believe that all the Allies were our enemies and would treat us very badly. It was propaganda like this that had inspired the German people to fight so bitterly to the end.

Eva saw how fearful I was. She couldn't pretend that our situation didn't look very bad but she tried to comfort me as much as she could. 'Don't worry, Puppe,' she said. 'They will know that we are not important to them. Look at us! Just a girl and a child. We'll be fine, I promise. But we must make sure they know that we are not going to resist. We have to carry white flags so they can see we surrender.'

We had already seen houses with white sheets draped from their windows. Eva broke two stout branches from a tree, and we tied the towel to one and Eva's white hankie to the smaller one. Eva told me to carry the smaller one over my shoulder, so that anyone approaching from behind would see my white flag. She did the same with the bigger one.

On we went, marching forward in the silence, carrying our flags of surrender. It seems almost funny now, to think that the Americans, with their might and weapons, would consider us a threat to them. But we truly believed that they would be monsters in human form, showing mercy to no German citizen, children included.

As we walked, we heard a distant rumble behind us, different from the throb of the heavy artillery. This was unrelenting, moving towards us, growing in volume.

'They're coming, Puppe!' gasped Eva, taking hold of my hand.

It was the invasion: the enemy were here. They were advancing upon us on the very road we were walking along. The sound of gunfire had gone, and through the still air the growl of the tanks and lorries could be heard for miles. Although they were easily half a mile away, the ground seemed to shake and the noise reverberated round the valley.

'Don't turn back, don't look at them,' Eva said,

clutching my hand very tightly. My heart was racing. 'Hold Charlotte, hope for the best and say a little prayer, and we'll be all right.'

I was terrified as the sound grew louder. We stepped off the road on to the grassy strip at the right-hand edge, among the fruit trees, which were brandishing their white blossom like our white flags, to make room for this strange new traffic that we dreaded. When it seemed the noise could get no louder and the whole world was shaking, a convoy of Sherman tanks came into view, rolling inexorably towards us.

Ignoring Eva's instructions, I looked up in awe as the huge caterpillar tracks thundered past. There were twenty or thirty tanks and it seemed to take for ever as they drove onwards, roaring by us in their ungainly way. When the last tank had lumbered past, there was a new procession of lorries and jeeps, which seemed ridiculously small and quiet compared with the slow beasts that had preceded them. In the back of the last lorry was a crowd of young men in American army uniform.

Here they were at last: the 'enemy' who had invaded our country.

To my surprise, they were not like the wicked monsters of my imagination at all. They didn't have two heads and horns. They weren't frightening. They weren't brandishing weapons or shouting abuse at us. All I could think was how they looked like our own soldiers, no different, except for the uniform.

They were grinning, laughing and waving at us. To my astonishment, they began to throw things out of the lorry to us – miniature bars of chocolate, small packs of biscuits and chewing gum.

The enemy, it turned out, consisted of friendly, young men, just like our soldiers. And that, as I was to learn, was the truth of it; the reality of war. Armies are made up of ordinary men, thrown into battle against each other through no fault of their own.

I sometimes wondered if any of these American soldiers, when they went back home, told their families about these two bedraggled creatures, a young woman and a small child, totally on their own on a deserted road, with little white flags over their shoulders. Despite their confidence and the military force they had behind them, these soldiers must have been apprehensive about what lay ahead. The war was not yet over and in some places the invading troops met with fierce fighting. I hope that we brought a smile to their faces and somehow touched their hearts. If we did, then we had done our little bit for peace.

Eva wrote in her diary later:

> I will never forget when we saw the first Americans. My heart was pounding in my throat and I dared not look at the cars and tanks, but when they started throwing goodies to us, my fears evaporated, bit by bit.

Further up the road the convoy had stopped and we caught up with them. Eva spoke a little English, so we were able shyly to say 'hello' and 'how are you'.

The American soldiers had jumped down from their tanks and lorries, and they ruffled their hands through my curly hair and one of them gave me a big wink.

The soldiers had set up folding trestle tables and

benches at the side of the road, and they invited us to sit with them and share their food. Gratefully, we joined them and had a meal of potato mash, corn and chicken, which was delicious. They were all very friendly and introduced themselves by their first names, which was very strange to us, as in Germany we were much more formal. We communicated through gestures and facial expressions, as well as Eva's bit of English. When we went on our way, they also gave us more goodies to take with us.

The smell of this part of my journey is the sweet, slightly sickly smell of bright pink gum, which I had never seen before. I chewed my first piece for ages, trying to make it small enough to swallow, before Eva explained that you didn't do that. She said, 'You're not meant to swallow it. In fact, if ever you swallow chewing gum, a rubber tree will grow inside you.'

I remembered a rubber plant we had back in our Hamburg flat, a monstrous triffid of a plant, which grew as tall as the room and branched out across the top of the window frame. I surely didn't want something like that inside me, so from then on I was always very circumspect with chewing gum.

We walked on, there were Americans all around us. We were wildly happy and sang loudly in our joy. All that horrible fear that we had travelled with for days had evaporated.

'See, it was good that we said a prayer,' said Eva, her face light and happy.

All I could feel was a huge sense of relief. We weren't going to be killed, or taken prisoner as I had feared. We were going to keep on walking, to find my Mutti.

––––––

We saw plenty more Americans as we approached Kirchhasel, and as we walked along the verge we found more food that they had thrown out to other refugees, but which had been missed. We filled our bags with biscuits and chocolate. In the village, which was draped with white flags, we went as usual to the community hall and were allocated an address where we could spend the night.

There was an overwhelming sense of relief among the other travellers and the people organising the billets. Grown-ups shook hands, lots of people patted me on the head or pinched my cheeks. Yes, we were a defeated nation, but we were drained and tired and just glad it was all over, and we exulted in the feeling of release.

As the Americans and British swept into Germany, they tried to do as little damage as possible. They did not want to carry on fighting; they, too, were desperate for an end to the war. They met some pockets of resistance and where this happened they crushed it ruthlessly, and there were villages and small towns where much destruction occurred. But resistance was rare and most places were left intact and the people unharmed. These soldiers wanted, above all, to survive themselves: death or injury at the moment of victory seemed horribly pointless.

If you travel through this beautiful area of Germany today, you will see the medieval town centres, untouched by the wars of the twentieth century. The people who live there are much more affected by years of Soviet domination, after their area was allocated to the Russians three months later, when Germany was partitioned among the Allies. They were not reunited with the rest of

Germany until 1990 and those years under Communist rule were very hard.

On the whole, the American troops entered towns and villages seeking a peaceable surrender. As the convoys of tanks and lorries approached a town, they would halt and an amplifier would warn the inhabitants, in German, not to resist. Usually the mayor and the head of the local troops would come forward with white flags, and the village would surrender. Often, they would then telephone ahead to arrange the surrender of the next village along the road.

Where there were SS troops and where, so sadly, there were the indoctrinated young boys of the Hitler Youth brigades, there might be defiance and a determination to obey Hitler's command to defend Germany to the death. These were the towns and villages that were inevitably destroyed by the tanks. Sometimes, in the distance, we would see the sky glowing bright orange, and we knew that a village had refused to surrender and was now ablaze.

For the most part, though, common sense and a strong desire to live and get back to some sort of normality prevailed. It soon became clear that the conquering army was not interested in reprisals. The devils that the Nazi propaganda had created in our heads did not exist, and as soon as we could see they were human beings who, like us, wanted peace and an end to the madness that had gripped the world for so long, we felt nothing but relief. For me, at only seven years old, there was no real understanding of the big world picture, the politics of defeat and victory. I did not know why all this was happening: like every child, what I needed and wanted was warmth, food and love. If Eva felt any shame at our country's defeat, she did not express it, either to me or in her diary. The nation was beyond that kind of pride, we had had it beaten out of us by years of war, a war that had been of our leader's making.

But not all our conquerors acted in this humane and dignified way. The Soviet troops behaved savagely and to this day I thank God that we were in the area of the country that was taken by the Americans, not in the path of invading Russians. They were desperate for revenge and took out their anger on everyone who crossed their path, man, woman or child. I know there have been stories of looting and even rape by British and American soldiers, but they are few and far between, and we never saw any of it. Our experience of the Allies was only good.

It's possible that, as a little curly-haired child, I was made a fuss of and only saw the best of everyone, but I don't think I was given any kind of preferential treatment. These soldiers who came in with their tanks and their guns were fine young men who wanted to get home to their wives and families, and they did not hold us, the women and children and old people who were left in the villages and towns, responsible for keeping them away overseas for so long.

They must have seen terrible things that would haunt them for the rest of their lives, just as I have never been able to forget the sight of bodies splayed in death by the sides of the road, or completely rid my nostrils of the stench. Some of these soldiers had the appalling task of liberating the concentration camps, and there is nothing I can say but to ask forgiveness for the atrocities committed in our name by our mad leader and his henchmen. But these men, the invading troops, never to my knowledge took it out on innocent Germans. They saw us, as we saw them within minutes of their arrival, as fellow human beings, thrust together by the appalling circumstances of war.

———————

If ever I needed proof that there are good and bad in all races, it came that night. The address we were given for our billet was of a house just beyond the centre of the village. It was a tall, fine-looking building with a big red front door, which I particularly remember. When we knocked we were let in by a very thin, nervous woman, who told us to come through into the kitchen and wait for her husband to come home.

We sat down at the kitchen table, but were not offered anything to eat or drink.

'May we have a glass of water, please?' Eva asked politely.

The woman nodded, fetched it for us silently and went back to her work. She was peeling a pan of potatoes and leeks, which she put on the large range to boil. We tried to chat to her, but she replied monosyllabically. She did not appear to share the

Barbie's parents, Norma & Waldemar on their wedding day, 5th October 1922.

Left to right: Eva, Barbie, Mutti & Ruth, 1942.

Barbie (*left*) & her best friend from Kindergarten, Inge, celebrating Mother's Day. Hamburg, 1942.

Barbie and Lumpie, her beloved puppy given to her by her father as a parting gift before he left to fight on the Russian front. Wartegau, 1944.

Barbie aged 4, topping and tailing gooseberries on the balcony of their apartment in Hamburg, 1942.

The brick factory house at Wartegau, 1944. *Left to right back row:* Mutti, Eva, Aunt Irma, Aunt Hilda. *Left to right front row:* Barbie, Henning, Volker.

Barbie in her red cardigan with the mother-of-pearl buttons and the red and white head scarf that just months later she was to wear on the trek with Eva. Lissa, Poland, 1944.

Eva wearing the ski clothes that she would later wear on the trek with Barbie. Tabarz, 1944.

The diary Eva wrote in throughout their trek and the little train given to Barbie by Miss Ramelow in Tabarz.

Inside pages of Eva's diary showing her entry for what she called their 'war Christmas, 1944' and Barbie's Christmas card to Eva: *Luttens erster brief* – 'the little one's first letter'.

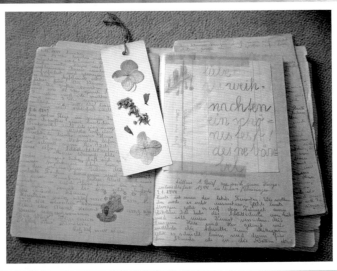

Eva & Kurt on their wedding day, 29th November 1947.

Barbie in the sandals made for her by Kurt, outside Caspar Voght High School, Hamburg, 1948.

Father lighting the candles on the tree, Hamburg, Christmas, 1960.

Barbie at university in Geneva, 1961.

Barbie with baby Meiki, 1964.

Left to right: Eva, Mutti and Barbie celebrating Mutti's 70th birthday, 22nd April 1974.

Barbie in the national German costume & her husband Ray in the uniform of Her Majesty's Band of the Welsh Guards, August 1981.

Meiki in his Springfield police uniform outside his home, The Firehouse, late 1997.

Left to right: Amy-Lou, Graham, AJ, Ray, Babs & Barbie, Christmas Eve, 2005.

general feeling of excitement that the war was finally over and she certainly did not want to engage in any discussion of it.

After half an hour or so of this stilted attempt at conversation, Eva was about to ask if we could be shown to where we would be sleeping, as it did not seem as if we were going to be given any food and we were both very tired. It had been a very long day, and we were physically and emotionally exhausted. Fortunately – and unusually – we were not terribly hungry, because we had eaten the American chocolate and biscuits.

At that moment the back door was flung open and a large red-faced man came in. We recognised him because he had been one of the people at the town hall, allocating the rooms.

'Ah, my two pretty girls,' he said when he saw us. 'You found the house all right? Is my wife looking after you? Has she prepared a meal for you?' He shot a glance at the woman, who scuttled around finding plates and knives and forks, and setting them down in front of us.

'Come, I shall sit between you and you can tell me the story of your lives,' the man said.

His wife put a bottle of beer down in front of him without speaking.

'Beer for the young lady. Don't you know how to treat guests?' he barked at his wife, who went to the larder and produced another bottle.

'No, thank you,' said Eva rather stiffly. I glanced at her and could tell she was not comfortable. The man leaned over me and touched my cheek.

'You're going to be a real beauty one day, just like your sister,' he said, turning to Eva. He rested his beefy arm along the back of her chair. 'So, where are you two going?'

We normally shared our story with any strangers we met, but I stayed silent, sensing Eva's concerns.

'Halle,' she replied and gave no further explanation.

'Trying to find your boyfriend, no doubt. A pretty girl like you has lots of boyfriends, I'm sure. I bet there are lots of men after you.'

Eva did not say anything, and just then the thin woman placed dishes of leeks and potatoes in front of us. There was also sausages, streaky bacon and bread on the table. The food silenced the man, as he fell upon it hungrily. The woman sat silently at her end of the table. Eva and I picked at our food; it was unappetising and we were both unnerved by the beery advances of the man.

As soon as he had mopped his plate with a thick slice of bread, he turned his attention back to Eva. His arm went along the back of her chair again. 'Now, you were telling me about your love life . . .' As he said this, his arm slipped down on to her shoulder.

Eva jumped up, pushing her chair back. 'Don't you touch me,' she said angrily. 'Puppe, get your things, we are leaving.'

'Don't do that. I was only being friendly. Just thought we could celebrate the end of the war, relax and have a drink together.' The man was wheedling, but Eva was busy collecting our bags. I picked up Charlotte and we headed for the door.

'You won't find anywhere else to stay tonight. The accommodation office is closed. It's too late. You've got to stay here.' This time the man sounded surly.

'We'll manage,' said Eva shortly.

The man got up and put his arm across the doorway. Eva turned to him, her eyes blazing. I had never seen her as angry as this before. 'Let us out,' she said in a voice of quiet fury and great power.

He leered at her, then reluctantly lowered his arm. He said something abusive, which I did not understand and Eva never explained to me. But as we left Eva turned to the woman and said, 'I feel sorry for you. Thank you for the meal and good luck.'

We walked out into an entirely dark, moonless night. After we had gone a few yards Eva stopped and bent down, facing me. 'I'm sorry, Puppe, but we just could not stay there. That is a very nasty man. Don't worry, we'll find somewhere to sleep.'

I didn't mind. I hadn't liked it in that house one bit. There was an atmosphere of fear and menace that I picked up on at once, even if I didn't understand it. I was just glad that Eva and I were out of there safely. It seemed that for every happy, wholesome experience we had, there was some darkness as well.

Even the events of this evening could not dim our overall happiness at the end of the war, though. The Americans were here – what we had dreaded had happened and it was actually the best thing we could have hoped for. We got out the torch, no longer frightened that its light would draw fire on to us, and continued along the road.

'We should keep going in the right direction, not go backwards,' said Eva.

Before long we came to a farm track and we could see a house about 200 yards down it. There were lights on, so we decided to take a chance and knock. The door opened a crack, a face peered out at us and the door was flung wide. 'Have to be careful,' said a cheerful voice. 'Come on in, you look like two lost orphans.'

This woman was also small and thin, but could not have been more different from her neighbour. She was cheerful and open, and welcomed us into the warm farmhouse. She and her husband shared their meal with us, and they produced a bottle of brandy so that they and Eva could toast the end of the war that would now surely come quickly, and peace. We told them all about our journey and Eva showed them her map.

'Here,' said the farmer. 'I've got a much better one than that.' He got it out and we all bent over it, to make out the route. 'You still have another seventy kilometres to get to Halle. Then a little bit further still to reach Wiedersdorf, where your mother is.'

Another forty-two miles at least to walk. We had gone out of our way so many times that we had already travelled over 100 miles, sometimes in the opposite direction to where we wanted to go, but we hadn't been able to take a direct path because of the fighting. At least the way would be clearer now and there was more behind us than there was in front.

The farmer's wife kept looking at me and clucking, 'Poor little thing!' She seemed to think it was far too far for me to have to walk.

We told her how we had lost our little cart, which at least had helped us carry our bags. At that, the farmer jumped up and went outside, declaring, 'I've got it!'

His wife laughed affectionately. 'Let's see what brilliant plan he has now,' she said.

When he returned, he told us to go to the door and parked outside was a large old-fashioned wooden wheelbarrow. 'Here you are,' he said. 'You can carry all your things in here and the little one can have a ride when she is too tired to walk!'

'What a wonderful idea!' cried Eva, delighted. 'Thank you so much, it will be so useful.'

Then he added, 'But there's a price to pay. Wheelbarrows don't come cheap.'

For a second Eva looked flustered. She still had some of Mutti's money, because most of the people we met along the way refused payment. Then she realised that the farmer was grinning.

'You've told us about how you sing to keep your spirits up. Now you can sing for us. Sing to earn yourselves a wheelbarrow.'

We all laughed, then Eva looked at me and whispered, 'Stille Nacht'. It was a tune we had been taught to sing in harmony.

So there we were, in the middle of April, in the last few days of the Second World War, singing the Christmas carol 'Silent Night' to a farmer and his wife, who had helped two young ones on their journey home. The kind couple had tears running down their cheeks. It was a very special, beautiful moment.

They only had a small spare bedroom with a single bed in it, but Eva and I were more than happy to share. We cuddled up together and went to sleep, glad to have escaped another nasty encounter and to have had our faith in human nature restored so quickly. Later, we wondered if the 'nasty man' (which was how we always referred to him) had deliberately selected us to be billeted in his house because he fancied Eva. We felt very sorry for his wife, as well as angry with her for not helping us. But perhaps she had had every ounce of resistance beaten out of her. She certainly seemed cowed, like an animal who has been harshly treated for a long time and has given up.

That night, before she dropped off to sleep, Eva wrote in her diary a quotation she remembered from the German poet Christian Morgenstern:

Go on God's path,
Don't let anyone else guide you away from it.
That way, you will go true and straight,
Even though you are on your own.

11

In Sight of Wiedersdorf at Last

We set off again the next morning, Eva pushing our new wheelbarrow. It was terribly heavy, but it did mean that we could keep going, even when my short legs needed a break. Once I told Eva to sit in it so I could push her. She climbed in, but of course I couldn't even lift it, which made Eva laugh.

The farmer and his wife had given us provisions: bread, cheese, a bottle with water in it. They also gave us a large Metwurst, which is a German sausage, like salami. We were delighted with it.

'You know what, Puppe?' asked Eva. 'We could

keep the Metwurst as a birthday present for Mutti. Her birthday is on 22 April and that is only five days away. We are sure to be with her by then. The farmer said we have only forty-two miles to go and I'm certain we can do that. What do you think?'

I thought it was a splendid idea. Not only would Mutti be delighted to see us, but we would have a lovely present for her too. I couldn't wait for that day to come. Just looking at the Metwurst and imagining Mutti's joy made me want to start running.

We must have looked a strange sight as we trundled on with our heavy barrow. It was a great bonus that we could now travel again in the daylight. Since the invasion, there was no fear that we would be fired at, and we could walk easily along the most direct route and the biggest roads that we'd had to avoid before. From now on our path would be straightforward and that alone put a spring in our steps.

We went on towards the city of Jena. As we approached, I became tired and for the last quarter of a mile or so Eva pushed me in the barrow. As usual, she made a game of it, telling me I was a princess in my carriage. It must have been back-breaking for her, but she never showed the strain to me.

Jena is a long-established city, dating back to before the founding of the world-renowned university there in the sixteenth century. It is built in the valley that the River Saale has been eating out of the limestone hills for thousands of centuries, and is famous today, as it was then, for its Zeiss optical factory. As we walked in, we had our first experience of how devastating the bombing had been in major cities. We knew about the bombing of Hamburg, but we had not seen it first hand. It seemed impossible to believe that anyone could have survived among these derelict buildings, but we soon realised that people were living in the debris of the shattered city.

Cellars were occupied and some buildings had been crudely restored on the ground floor only. There was row upon row of blackened shells that were once houses, shops and factories, tottering against each other, like drunkards holding one another up.

We were looking for the place that would give

us a billet for the night, so we headed towards a large park in the centre of the city, which in peacetime must have been a beautiful spot. American soldiers were setting up camp there and it was bustling with life, as men in the still unfamiliar US uniform rushed about.

Exhausted, Eva was struggling to push me in the wheelbarrow when a large American GI came over to us. He was very tall, a giant to me, but even more astonishing was the colour of his skin. I had never seen a black person before in my life and I didn't know whether to be frightened or fascinated. Then I remembered Eva telling me that I must never let my reactions show on my face, whatever people looked like, as it might hurt their feelings, so I tried to look and stay calm. 'Always be nice and kind to every creature there is,' Eva said, but I was so astonished I literally held my breath. The only black people I had ever seen were piccaninnies in a fairy tale book and I was awestruck by the smooth, shiny handsomeness of this stranger.

With gestures and speaking in English, the soldier told us to sit down on a bench. Eva could understand enough of what he was saying, so we obeyed.

I clambered out of the wheelbarrow, clutching Charlotte, and he took our bags out and put them on the ground near us.

He said, 'Stay there. I'll be back.' Then he grabbed the handles of our heavy wheelbarrow and pushed it effortlessly away. Eva and I looked at each other, not knowing what to think. Perhaps he had taken our wheelbarrow because he needed it for something. We had no idea, but we felt we had no choice in the matter. Although every American we had encountered so far had been friendly, we were still acutely aware that they were now our bosses.

I cannot say how long we sat there. It could have been twenty minutes, maybe half an hour. We were tired, so the chance to sit down was appreciated. Then we saw the big man approaching again with his long, loping stride. In front of him, instead of our wheelbarrow, he was pushing a large pram, one of the old-fashioned coachworked prams that people had in those days. It was a big, well-sprung, expensive one. As he brought it up to us, the soldier gestured that we should look inside. Peering over the edge, we saw that it was full of goodies for us – sweets, chocolate, army rations, tea bags. As our eyes grew wide with amazement, he held his arms out to me, picked me up, swung me up into the air and down into the pram. His face was split by the most enormous smile, showing two rows of immaculately white teeth. Impulsively, I stretched up my arms and hugged him. He chuckled, ruffled my hair, saluted us, then turned away and went back to the camp.

We were thrilled. From starting out in fear of our GI, we had come to see him as one of the kindest people we had ever met. We will never know whether he exchanged the wheelbarrow for the pram, or how he acquired it, but it made such a difference to us. Now Eva could push me so easily, without really feeling my weight unless she was pushing up a steep hill. (It is a tribute to the craftsmanship of those days that a pram designed for a baby could support the weight of a seven-year-old girl, even if I was very skinny and underweight at the time. I don't think many of today's pushchairs would be up to it.)

We found the refugee point and were allocated our billet on a farm just outside the city, so we set off towards it, with me in my luxurious pram stuffed with lovely things. Among the treasure we found were a banana and an orange. I had never seen a banana before and at first I tried to eat it with the skin on. Eva laughed and showed me how to peel it. I could only vaguely remember ever having an orange and we hadn't seen any of those for the past three years or so. We peeled it carefully and had half each, and felt we were enjoying a real feast.

We arrived at our billet, which was a farm run by a woman on her own. She didn't seem to have a husband, or perhaps he was away at the war, and she took us into the *Räucherkammer*, the smoke room, where all the bacon and sausages were preserved. The smell of smoked meat always evokes memories of this room, although there were many other intermingled scents. In a smoke room the fire is left to smoulder on, fed with juniper berries, bay leaves and other herbs to flavour the huge sides of bacon and rings of sausages hanging above from the rafters. Naturally, we ate sausage that evening and enjoyed a comfortable night's sleep.

The next morning we were up early, eager to press on. With the pram, we could move much faster. I walked for as long as I could, until I was too tired to go on, then Eva could push me quite comfortably. This, coupled with the lack of fighting on the roads, meant that we made very good progress. It really felt as though we would reach Mutti soon and were on the last leg of our long journey.

We bypassed the towns of Apolda, Bad Sulza and Naumburg, on Eva's list of our route, which she had carefully written out in her diary in case we lost the map. By the evening, we had reached Weissenfels, and here Eva had a letter to deliver to a lady doctor from one of the other members of staff at the home in Tabarz.

That night we stayed with a lovely lady who, like so many people, was desperate for news of her family, all of whom were caught up in the war. She made us very welcome and we had a relaxing evening in her company. She, like us, came from Hamburg, and she told us her house there was still intact and that we were welcome to stay there as long as we needed to when we finally got back to the city. It was a very generous offer because we were complete strangers and she had no idea how trustworthy we were. She insisted on Eva taking a note of her address in the city, just in case we needed it. Our hostess and Eva spent the evening nostalgically discussing the old Hamburg, remembering shops and churches and other places they had both visited. My memories, of course, were much more limited, centring as they did around our old apartment and the nursery school. But our hostess knew the Wandsbecker Chaussee, where we lived, and could even more or less pinpoint our block, because she remembered the bakery on the ground floor. We slept well and set off later than usual the next day. Our wonderful hostess gave us cheese and sugar drops to take with us on our journey.

We walked on to Merseburg, which was only about ten miles away. Because it was a relatively short distance, I walked the whole way while Eva pushed the pram. It seems incredible now that we walked such distances and it is a testament to how well shoes were made, because we never had trouble with our feet. It was my legs that ached, sometimes so badly that it was hard to get to sleep. Eva continued to massage them, and to sing and tell me stories to relax me. Every night, unless I was so tired I fell asleep before we could do it, we said prayers, always for our mother and especially for our father, because it was so long since we had heard from him. We also prayed for our sister Ruth in heaven, our grandparents and the rest of the family, and I often found myself wondering what my cousins, Volker and little Henning, were doing. The long, perfect days of play with Volker when we lived near the brick factory seemed a lifetime ago, although in fact it was only three months since we had left. It was as if that world had come out of one of the story books we used to read. My reality was here and now, on the road, existing from day to day, never knowing what tomorrow might bring.

———

Merseburg had been badly damaged by bombs. It was by far the worst we had seen, worse than Jena. The city was home to a large oil works, which produced the high-quality aviation fuel needed by the *Luftwaffe* to fly their planes. This made it a major target for the Allies and from May 1944 to the end of that year there were more than a dozen bombing raids on Merseburg. Sixty-five per cent of the population had been killed and there was a dispirited feeling to the whole place.

We picked our way through rubble and debris, past blackened scars where houses and apartment blocks had stood, with Eva struggling to push our pram along roads that had not been cleared, where not a single building was left standing. The absence of buildings made the roads seem strangely wide, without definition, and they were strewn with debris, including electrical cables (which Eva made me keep well away from), broken glass and remains of furniture. Where walls had collapsed there was a view like an architectural cross-section of a building, with half-rooms on show at every floor level, furniture still intact, tables with crockery on and curtains across windows.

Nevertheless, the city was reviving a little and we saw a few makeshift shops, nothing more than roadside stalls, and women in headscarves scurrying about their business. There was still a tremendous air of desolation and we were not able to find any central arrangements for dealing with refugees.

We still had a little food left from the rations we had been given by the Americans, but not much. We sat on the remains of a wall and ate it. Throughout our walk we were very lucky with the weather and we watched a lovely sunset over the jagged ruins of the city.

As dusk fell, Eva started to become anxious. 'Come on,' she said. 'We must find somewhere sheltered to sleep. There's no one to organise anything for us, so I think we'll be looking after ourselves tonight.'

She did not say anything but I could tell that she was worried about the scavengers we saw, people who were trying to eke out their survival from nothing and prowled about the ruins of the buildings looking for anything they could use. There was no doubt that we had some treasures with us, with our pram and our rucksacks, and Eva was apprehensive that we would have our things stolen if we didn't find somewhere safe.

A young woman approached us and introduced herself, in the formal German way, as Miss Reinhardt. She was older than Eva, probably in her mid twenties and, like us, a refugee trying to get to her home. 'Where are you heading?' she asked. She seemed friendly enough.

'Halle,' said Eva.

'I'm off to Leipzig. Quite the other way. But it

looks like we're all going to be spending a night in Merseburg, doesn't it? Why don't we stick together? I'm sure we'll all be safer that way.'

Eva agreed, pleased to have an ally. We walked on, the two of them constantly looking for a place where we might shelter for the night. It was 20 April, twelve days after we had set off, and the nights were still chilly, so we needed to find cover if we could. After a few hundred yards one of them spotted a cellar and we explored it. The house above had been demolished but we could pick our way through piles of bricks and timber to the steps that led down into the dry cellar. This, they decided, would be our best place to stay. We hauled our precious pram down the steps, put on our extra jumpers and settled in for the night. There was nowhere to sit or lie except the hard floor, which was cold, but we had no choice. I lay with my head on my little pink rucksack and slept. Eva and Miss Reinhardt, with their backs propped against the wall, were only able to doze. They talked for a while, then slept as best they could.

Shortly after dawn I was flung awake by Eva jerking forward and letting out a howl of pain. A piece of masonry from the derelict building above us had broken free and fallen, hitting her on the head. There was a lot of blood, which we staunched with our hankies and the towel.

I was very worried and almost in tears to see my beloved sister injured like this; the sight of the blood pouring from her head was terrifying.

'Now don't worry,' she kept saying. 'It looks much worse than it is. I'm going to be all right.'

Later she wrote in her diary, 'I was so glad it didn't hit Puppe.'

The two of them immediately decided the cellar was not safe and that we should get help for Eva if we could. So between the three of us we dragged the pram up to the road and set off. Eva walked behind, holding the towel to her head. A woman in the street directed us to a medical centre and we were lucky to find a nurse on duty despite the earliness of the hour. She reassured us that it was not a deep wound and applied a neat bandage round Eva's forehead.

While we were in the medical centre, we were also able to use the bathroom, so we could clean ourselves up with our lavender soap, which we loved because it left its lingering fragrance on our skins. We washed our blood-soaked towel and hankies, as we knew we still needed them.

Eva wrote in her diary that for days afterwards she had 'terrible headaches', but she never mentioned anything that would worry me, and whenever I asked her about her wound she just laughed and made a joke about her 'battle scars'.

It was 11 a.m. before we went on our way again. We said goodbye to Miss Reinhardt, who went off to Leipzig, and Eva and I headed north-west. We were really excited because we knew we were getting close to where we had parted from our mother all that time ago. We were only about ten miles from Halle and Wiedersdorf was not much further.

As we walked out of Merseburg, Eva told me the fairy story about the raven that stole the bishop's ring. I'd heard it before, but it was a thrill to me to know that I had spent the night in the town where it was set. An innocent man was imprisoned and executed for stealing the ring, before it was eventually uncovered in the raven's nest. For that reason, at the city's castle, a raven is still to this day kept in a cage as a punishment for the sin of its ancestor. When I was smaller I would have felt a cold chill at the idea of anyone being put to death, for whatever reason. But now, death was all around me and I had seen more bodies of innocent people than I had of those whose war crimes justified their execution. Nevertheless, one man, wrongly put to death centuries ago, still moved me. I loved the story about the bird. One day I would like to re-create the journey that Eva and I made, and if I do I will visit the raven at Merseburg.

Today, Merseburg is a satellite town of Halle and the road between the two is apparently built up. Sixty years ago there were still fields for us to walk beside, although the wooded hillsides were dropping away from us. By mid afternoon, to our great excitement, we could see Halle ahead of us. It was a city, largely undamaged by bombing, on the other bank of the River Saale, whose course we had been shadowing for many miles and many days since we first encountered it at Rudolstadt.

But, to our frustration and despair, we could not get to it. The bridges across the river had been blown up to halt the Allied progress. We walked about for a while, feeling increasingly desperate. Then we saw a bridge, but when we got to it Eva realised that it was a railway bridge. 'That's no good,' she cried. 'We can't cross on a railway. It's impossible. What on earth are we going to do?'

We would have to walk miles in either direction to find a place to get across the river. We must have looked desolate, because eventually three men approached us.

'Are you trying to get over the river?' asked one.

'Yes,' said Eva warily, holding my hand tightly. But her fears soon disappeared as they turned out to be very kind. They were not dressed in uniform even though they looked young enough to have been called up towards the end of the war. We will never know who they were or what they were doing. In those difficult days nobody asked questions that could embarrass others.

They explained that they were going to cross the railway bridge and they would help us. We accepted their offer gratefully.

First we had to scramble up a steep embankment to get to the railway. The men helped us up. One got to the top and stretched his arm down, while another of them literally handed me up to him. I was all skin and bones, no weight at all. Then they helped Eva to scrabble her way up the steep, scrubby ground. Finally, they dragged our pram up.

At the top we were on the railway track and I looked nervously up and down it.

'You don't need to worry, young miss,' said one, laughing when he saw my face. 'There's no danger from trains. There aren't any running in Germany any more. Come on, let's get going.'

Even though I knew that there were no longer any trains steaming their way along the rails, it was nonetheless alarming to walk along a gleaming, well-used railway line, now pitched at a groggy angle because of bomb damage. The Saale is a wide river and the drop from the bridge to the water was great. Eva and I are not good with heights, and the parapets at the side of the bridge were low and distorted. Once we had left the relative safety of the bank behind and were out over the murky water far below we were terrified and almost frozen to the spot.

One of the men coaxed us along. 'Get down on your hands and knees and crawl,' he said kindly.

'That's the way to do it.' Putting Eva ahead of me, he said to her, 'I am just in front of you, and you must keep your eyes on me and nothing else. Don't look to your left or right.'

To me he said very gently, 'Watch your sister's bottom.'

I giggled when he said what seemed to me to be a rude word and he grinned, probably glad to have relieved my tension.

'Don't take your eyes off it. Crawl behind it all the way and before very long we'll be on the other side. I promise.'

One of the other men added, 'And we'll be right behind you. We won't let anything happen to you, we promise. We'll be following your bottom.'

He said it deliberately, to make me smile again.

Then we set off in our bizarre little convoy. The first man crawled and we crawled after him. It was difficult going, lifting our hands and knees from railway sleeper to railway sleeper. Behind us, the other two men stayed upright but close, and they spoke calmly and encouragingly to us. They were carrying our pram between them, as it was impossible to push it. The journey seemed to take for ever as we progressed slowly, inch by inch, but eventually we reached the other side. We had crossed the great river, crawling on our hands and knees along a railway.

The leader of our convoy jumped down from the track and held up his arms to Eva, who fell into them. When she was safe, he and the man behind me together lifted me down the embankment to the road. Our hands were red-raw sore and we had splinters in them from the wooden sleepers. Our knees were sore, too, and our trousers were practically worn through. But we were delighted. A really difficult part of our journey was over and we were ever closer to Mutti.

We thanked the men profusely, but they did not hang around. Whoever they were, and wherever they were going, they were again intent on their own affairs. We found ourselves in Ammendorf, an industrial town that has now been virtually absorbed into Halle. It is famous as a railway town, where rolling stock is manufactured. During the war, it was where the special carriages used to transport people to the concentration camps were made.

As usual, we made our way to the town hall and

were given an address as a billet for the night. I know exactly where we stayed because Eva made a note of it in her diary: Hallischestrasse 107 and the name of the man whose family put us up was Schneider. She even recorded that his title was *Diplomingenieur*, which means he was a senior engineer in one of the factories in the town.

Once again we were in luck. It was a wonderful billet. The family were very welcoming. We had a bath – our first since we left Tabarz – and a lovely meal of curly kale with smoked sausages and potatoes, and afterwards a fresh fruit compote with vanilla sauce. When you don't eat often, food becomes very important and I remember these wartime meals vividly. They tasted better than anything I have ever eaten since, even food served by five-star restaurants.

Just as wonderful were the clean sheets we slept in that night. You can only appreciate fresh linen fully if you have gone for days sleeping, at best, in beds others have already slept in and, at worst, in barns and cellars. The one thing that kept me awake was my excitement at being so close to our goal. The next day was 22 April, our mother's forty-first birthday, and it was the day we would be reunited with her. It felt as though all my birthdays and Christmases were coming at once and if I had not been so physically exhausted, I don't think I would have slept a wink.

Next morning we put on our clean underwear, thrilled that even though our outer clothes were very grubby, we were as clean as we could be for Mutti. We still had our Metwurst, our present for her, and we were really proud of ourselves for having a gift, despite the circumstances.

We started walking early, anxious to get to her. We sang happy songs as we marched along, following roads that skirted the city of Halle and took us to Wiedersdorf, where we had last seen our mother and said goodbye to her before the journey to Tabarz. I was skipping with excitement and Eva had to tell me to slow down or I would be too tired for the walk.

We got as far as the village of Kochwitz, and we could see Wiedersdorf in the distance. Then we saw two young girls, aged about fourteen, coming towards us, and as they came closer we realised that we knew them. They were called Anke and Jutta, and they lived in Wiedersdorf, in the same street as the house where our family was staying. I knew them because I spent a couple of weeks there and even Eva had chatted to them before, during the two days she stayed when she picked me up to go to Tabarz. They recognised me straight away because of my curly blonde hair.

We smiled and greeted them.

'What are you doing here?' asked Anke.

'We've come to meet our mother, of course. We're on our way to the headmaster's house now, to see her.'

They stared at us with wide, solemn eyes. 'Don't you know, then?'

My stomach dropped with fear and I could feel Eva tense. 'Know what?' she asked in a frozen voice.

'Your mother's gone. She left days ago, when the last train departed for Hamburg. Lots of people got on it when they found out there would be no more trains.' Seeing our stunned faces, the girls looked concerned. 'We're sorry to tell you the bad news. Are you all right?'

We were not all right. There are no words to express what we felt. The shock was almost too great to take in. We sat down by the roadside and cried and cried and cried. It was as if everything had been taken away from us. We had been through so much to get to her and it was the thought of her that had kept us going. Whenever I was low and tired, Eva had always told me how close we were getting to Mutti and she would build a picture for me of us all living together again. For the last two or three days we had been literally counting off the miles. It was the thought of Mutti's face that gave me the courage to crawl across the railway bridge and whenever we felt like giving up it was her voice we heard in our heads, urging us onwards.

But she wasn't there. Now what would we do?

12

Back on the Road

We walked on, numb and bewildered, to Wiedersdorf. What else could we do? We couldn't go back. We had been walking for two weeks and although, as the crow flies, we had only covered about seventy miles, the circuitous route we followed more than doubled that, and had taken us through rough and dangerous terrain. Through our many frightening experiences, what had kept us going was the thought of being reunited with our mother. It had sustained us through the blackest times and had made the final couple of days, as we neared our goal, a journey of joyful expectation.

We were desolate. I don't have the words to describe the depth of our misery. For once, Eva could not conceal from me that she was devastated. She wrote in her diary:

Nothing worse could have happened to us. All this for nothing. It was just like somebody was sticking a knife in my heart. The whole way, and now nothing. It couldn't be true. Mutti couldn't have gone without us. I just could not believe it. We cried and cried and cried.

We went to the house of the headmaster and his wife, where we had last seen our mother and where she stayed until she caught the train back to Hamburg. They were surprised to see us as well but could not have been more welcoming. The first thing they did was give us a letter that Mutti had left for us in case we turned up there looking for her. It was a small comfort to know that she had thought of us. Her letter had been written in haste:

My darling Eva and Bärbel,

We have all taken the last train back to Hamburg. I think it is better to try to find a home there, while we still have family and friends, than to stay here as lodgers, even though our hosts are very kind to us. Go to Aunt Käte's when you get to Hamburg: if I am not there, she will know where I am.

Lots of love, and God's blessing to keep you safe and well,

Mutti

It was wonderful to see Mutti's handwriting, and know she was thinking of us and sending her love to us, but it is hard to express how lonely we felt. The entire family – our grandparents, Aunt Irma and Henning, Aunt Hilda and Volker – had all gone, too. It was a bleak moment.

We were very low and our hosts set about trying to cheer us up, helping us to settle in and unload the pram. As I picked up the Metwurst I felt a surge of hatred for it. It was as if it were mocking me. We had made it in time for Mutti's birthday, but she was not here, so her present was pointless.

'I want to throw it away,' I said miserably. I didn't even want to look at it.

Eva stared at it for a moment, clearly with the same opinion of our sausage as mine. She held it out to our kind hosts. 'Would you like the Metwurst? It was going to be a present for Mutti. It's her birthday today.'

They politely declined. 'You should keep it for your mother,' they said. 'You will most certainly see her again.'

It was hard to recover from the massive disappointment that felt as though it had knocked us both to the ground. But our hosts did everything they could to raise our spirits, and they made sure that our creature comforts, at least, were catered for. They ran hot baths for us and we had the luxury of washing our hair with shampoo. That evening we sat down to a meal served with napkins, silver cutlery and a clean tablecloth. We were given some old clothes to wear while ours were taken from us, and washed and pressed and repaired.

Despite their kindness, it was hard for Eva and me to muster polite conversation, or recount the stories of our adventures, when our hearts felt like breaking. That night we slept in crisp linen sheets, but we dampened our clean pillows with our tears.

———————

The next morning we slept late. When I awoke, Eva was already up, sitting at the lovely dressing table in our bedroom, brushing her hair. She turned towards me with her usual big smile and said, 'Well, there's nothing for it, Puppe, but to carry on walking. We made it this far, we can make it the rest of the way.'

'Can we get a train, like Mutti?' I asked, even though I knew the answer.

'No, remember there are no more trains. Mutti and the others were on the very last one.'

'So we'll have to walk again?'

'Yes, but it will be much easier now the fighting is over. And we have our lovely pram, so I can push you the whole way if you like.'

She didn't tell me that 'the whole way' was another 200 miles, further than we had already come. Even so, I had no heart for walking any more. I was so sad that Mutti was not there that I couldn't imagine setting out again. How would we have the spirit for our walk? But as soon as I woke properly and saw how positive and cheerful Eva was, I agreed that we should press on. Eva wrote in her diary:

> *I decided there and then that I'll take my little Puppe and march on towards Hamburg.*

Her resilience was amazing. She had been unable to hide from me the acute misery of the previous day, but she was already looking on the bright side once more. Perhaps she felt there was no choice. It could take months, even years, to get a train service going again and the only thing we could do until then would be to stay in Wiedersdorf, lonely refugees far from our family and home, despite the kindness of our hosts. But even if Eva's decision to press on was born of necessity, she made it sound like fun and a good choice for us. 'We'll go tomorrow,' she said firmly. 'So enjoy your day here, Puppe. Let's make the most of it.'

For that day of respite we luxuriated in the kind hospitality of our hosts, taking more baths and being looked after with solicitous attention. The headmaster and his wife had become very fond of Mutti and the rest of our family, and although their slightly formal bearing meant I was in awe of them, they were transparently good-hearted and concerned about us.

They wanted us to rest for longer, but we were determined to get started. When the headmaster warned Eva about the dangers of a young woman and a child travelling alone, Eva reminded him of some of the situations we had already faced. 'Nothing could be worse than we've endured getting this far,' she said.

How I wish she had been right . . .

While we rested, our host made himself busy. That night we ate a feast. He'd killed and roasted one of their precious chickens especially for us, served with delicious bottled fruit from his cellar and a glass of wine for all the grown-ups.

'I can see that you are determined, Fraulein Eva,' the headmaster said as we finished off the wonderful dinner. 'I won't try and stop you. It says a great deal about your strength and will that you have got this far with Bärbel. It would be wrong to prevent you going to your mother when it means so much to you both. But I want you to agree to something. I know of two fellows who are setting off in the same direction as you tomorrow morning, and I'd like you to consider going along with them for as long as possible. They are sound men and I would feel better knowing you were with them, at least in the beginning. Would you do that?'

Eva agreed and we went upstairs for our last night in the cosy beds of the headmaster's house.

The next morning we were introduced to our travelling companions. The first was Mr Kramer, a man in his sixties who had not had to fight but had been drafted in to run a supply depot. He was tall, slightly stooped and very short-sighted. His glasses had such thick lenses you could see circles in them, and when he looked at you directly his eyes were enormous and seemed to swim behind the lenses, like a fish's eyes. I was fascinated by this and it was made especially bizarre by the fact that one lens was broken and held together with sticky tape, which obscured half his eye.

The other was Dr Hagen, who was, I think, in

his forties, although as a child it was hard to pin-point people's ages. They all seemed 'old' to me. I never found out what Dr Hagen had been doing during the war. He didn't talk about it. Perhaps he told Eva, but she never mentioned it, even when we talked about our long walk in the years to come. Perhaps he had been in the army and had simply avoided being taken prisoner, and was making his own way home. He was not in uniform, but I think many people helped soldiers by giving them civilian clothes to wear. I remember his trousers were much too big in the waist and he had a thick piece of rope holding them up. In civilian life, though, he had been a schoolteacher (in Germany, teachers often have the title Doctor) and was an old colleague of our host at Wiedersdorf. He and Mr Kramer were both making their way back to their homes to find their families.

The four of us set off on our journey, waving goodbye to the kind headmaster and his wife. Once again we were on the road with our pram and little rucksacks. I still kept Charlotte close to me at all times and this time we at least had a good supply of food. We had bread, cheese, ham, and some of the apples and pears that the headmaster and his wife had carefully preserved in their cellar. They also gave us some lovely warm blankets to take with us.

I remember leaving Wiedersdorf oblivious to the fact that this undertaking was going to be much harder than our first trek. We thought that now the war was almost over, life would be practically normal again. We didn't realise that, although the walking itself was easier and the route more direct, not only were we going much further than we had previously but that life in an occupied, starving country could have its own great perils and dangers.

On our first day we skirted Halle, going along the country lanes. Just as we had previously encountered the *Panzergraben* trenches, now we came across large piles of logs outside each village, makeshift roadblocks to slow down the invasion. Dr Hagen was stocky and strong, and whenever the logs blocked our way he set about clearing them off the road with remarkable ease, so we were lucky to have him with us.

We made really good progress, mainly because there were now three people to take turns at pushing me in the pram. There were no attacks, we could walk in daylight and we never got diverted from our route. There were more people travelling, and occasionally we fell in with others and walked a little way with them. It was a great relief not to be forced to leap into hedges or fling myself to the ground as bullets ricocheted around me.

But it was harder to find billets for the night. We avoided stopping in towns or big villages, because they were in chaos. The administration that had worked so well, with so much provision for refugees, had in many places broken down completely. The cities had no electricity supplies, the sewers were ruptured, there were homeless people everywhere and some had become ruthless in their bid for survival. Many of the top officials who had organised refugee billets were dead, or had fled. Often they simply killed themselves, knowing that their future as 'good' Nazis would be difficult, or because they were genuinely deluded into thinking that life without the Nazi machine would not be worth living. Their disappearance left a vacuum.

Even where there was some sort of local authority, the problems in the towns were far too great for them to worry about people like us, who were passing through.

Looting was rife and so was robbery. The major towns, in those few sombre days between the invasion and the official end of the war when temporary governance was assumed by the Allies, were dark, dangerous, lawless places. There were even women who felt they had no choice but to resort to prostitution as the only means to obtain food for themselves and their children. As the towns became more organised, curfews were imposed, sometimes for all but three hours of the day, in a bid to keep people off the streets to allow them to be cleared. When food supplies were resumed, ration cards were issued, but there was never any excess food for travellers like us.

On our first night we slept under the arch of a bridge crossing a small river, a tributary of the River Saale. We were still following the route of that river, but not for much longer. Eva knew that the Saale would eventually flow into the Elbe, and if we followed the Elbe north, we would reach Hamburg, but to go all the way with the Saale would have added miles to our route. The water level in this small river was low because there had been so little rain, and we were able to find two niches in the brickwork where we tried to make ourselves as comfortable as possible, Mr Kramer and Dr Hagen in one, and Eva and me in the other. Fortunately we had the blankets given to us by our hosts at Wiedersdorf, so we could wrap ourselves up and be quite snug. I loved that night, because there was a lot going on in the water. There were sounds of plopping and flopping all night. Perhaps it was fish, or maybe toads and frogs. I was half asleep and half awake, and for me it was like something from *Alice in Wonderland*. I could not see in the dark, but I imagined large frogs sitting on lily pads watching me. They didn't frighten me because I pretended that they were there to protect me. I love the sound of water and there was the constant babble of the little river, soothing and reassuring. I remember too the shrill sound of crickets in the hour before I dozed off – or perhaps they, like the frogs, were part of my dream.

The next day when we woke we called out 'Good

morning!' to the men in the next niche, and there was a beautiful echo. So I called out 'good morning' several times and my echoes mingled with the echoes of the men replying to me. It made me laugh.

After a small breakfast from our provisions, we returned to the road and continued walking on towards the town of Alsleben, where we needed to make our final crossing of the River Saale. When we got there, we found that we could not cross by the main Alsleben bridge because, like so many others, it had been destroyed by the retreating German army to halt the invasion.

We found a makeshift ferry operating, which we hoped would be able to take all four of us across. It was nothing more than a flat raft, with no sides, and getting on was a precarious undertaking, as it swayed and rocked underneath us. Not only that, but we had our beloved pram to take with us as well. Mr Kramer and Dr Hagen helped Eva manoeuvre it aboard.

'You should leave that thing behind,' said the ferryman sourly. But Eva insisted that it was coming with us and paid the surly man in advance. Once aboard, we had to huddle together in the middle even though I wanted to sit at the edge and trail my hands in the water.

'You must stay very still,' she told me sternly. I think she was afraid that any movement would topple the raft over.

Safely on the other side, we followed the main road on to Aschersleben. As we walked along, we came upon some parked trucks, and a group of American soldiers having a meal at the side of the road. They must have been a supply unit, following the main invasion army, because there were only lorries in the convoy, no tanks.

They greeted us cheerfully and we went up to talk to them. We were no longer afraid of these foreign soldiers: in the space of a few short days they had gone from being our enemies to being our friends.

'Why don't you join us for some food?' asked one, so we sat down and had some ham and crackers with them. They also had packs of instant Nescafé that came in their rations. I had no real memory of coffee, as we'd had none during the war years, but Eva and the two men were thrilled with it.

Afterwards they told me how it was a poor imitation of the real thing — before the war the only coffee that was drunk in Germany was filtered, made from freshly ground beans — but they were still glad to have it.

After the meal, the soldiers offered us a lift, which we gratefully accepted, so they loaded the pram into the back of one of their lorries and we climbed up. It reminded me of travelling with the German soldiers. The Americans made just as much fuss of me, and one of them pulled out his wallet to show me a picture of his daughter; she was pretty with curly hair like mine. Apart from the language difference and the uniform, they were so like the others, their 'enemy'. They were a happy bunch. I could not understand what they said, but they were laughing and joking, and were no doubt as relieved as we were that the fighting was over and we could all relax in each other's company. Dr Hagen, having been a teacher, could speak quite good English, so he did some translating and talked to them. The soldiers also chatted to Eva, although her English was more limited than Dr Hagen's, while Mr Kramer and I listened and tried to follow what was going on. Later, Dr Hagen told us that the soldiers were telling him which parts of America they were from and how long they had been away from home. Home was on everybody's lips at this time: it was where we all wanted to be and where we were all heading. For those of us who no longer had a physical home, it was where our family was.

Near Aschersleben our friends dropped us off with the extra gift of some supplies, ration packs all marked 'breakfast'. Presumably they had more of those than they did of the lunch and dinner packs. They also handed us even more chewing gum.

We walked into Aschersleben and went about the usual routine of locating the town hall and finding out what arrangements, if any, there were for refugees and travellers like us. Once we got there Mr Kramer, the joker with the broken glasses, left us. He had not seen his wife or his children, who had all been drafted into the army or the BDM, for many months, and now at last he was close to home, not far at all from the village where his family lived.

'Goodbye!' we all said. 'And good luck.'

He shook our hands. 'Good luck to you too. I hope you find your family safe and well.'

the other German romantic poets. So travelling with him helped continue my unofficial education.

Most of the time we lacked the means to boil water to make coffee or tea, but sometimes, in the villages, we could get some hot water. Increasingly we found that people were less hospitable, more suspicious, on this leg of our journey, and doors did not open for us as readily as they had before.

'You know, Puppe, I think we're going to be sleeping outside a bit more now,' said Eva. 'It's lucky that it's so fine, isn't it? At least the ground is dry. It will be fun, snuggling under our blankets and looking up at the stars, won't it? Just like camping.'

As usual, Eva looked on the bright side of every-thing for me. But on the next night we did find a billet, with a widow and her daughter who lived on the edge of a village. The widow saw us walking along and must have decided that we looked respectable enough, so she let Eva and me sleep in her house in armchairs. Dr Hagen was allowed to use a small barn where she had some chickens and a goat.

The daughter, Renate, was in her forties, and mildly mentally handicapped. She talked slowly and probably was mentally younger than I was. I remember easily beating her at draughts. Eva told me quietly that I should let her win occasionally, so I did. Renate laughed a lot, a sort of embarrassed giggly laugh, which was her way of making conversation, as she found speech difficult. Her mother was very pleased that I played with her and talked to her, as she did not have any friends.

'She is too old for children and too young for adults,' she said wistfully. I thought it was an odd remark, because at the time I did not appreciate the problems she must have faced looking after her daughter. She was very relieved that it was the Americans who had invaded this area, not the Russians.

'What would have happened to my poor Renate?' she kept asking. Again, I had no idea what she meant, except that I knew we were all glad not to be in the path of the Soviet troops.

Staying there was a pleasant interlude, despite our constant worry and anxiety about what lay ahead. Apart from her chickens and the goat, the widow had a large vegetable patch and we ate well: omelettes, potatoes, carrots and coffee made with the American packets. The widow, like us, had not tasted coffee for years. We used the goat's milk with it and I must admit it did taste very odd to me. I still rarely drink coffee — I'd much rather have a cup of tea.

The widow seemed to enjoy our company, and asked if we would like to stay and rest for a couple of days, but we thanked her and refused. We wanted to get on to Hamburg; that was all that mattered to us.

We set off the next day, and after a while we came into a village where we hoped to buy some bread and other supplies. Eva still had most of the money that Mutti had given her but she was shocked and dismayed at the prices being charged for everything. We walked out of the first baker's because Eva said it was too expensive, but in the end we found they were all charging the same amount, so we had to pay what they asked for a loaf and we bought some cheese. We were suffering from hunger much more on this second part of our trek. This close to defeat, and with all the normal systems of society breaking down, food supplies were increasingly scarce. And as Dr Hagen had no money at all, of course we shared all our food with him.

Back on the Road

After our expensive, but much needed, lunch the three of us, Eva pushing me in the pram and Dr Hagen walking with his doghead stick, carried on marching towards our destination.

13

The Boys from the Hitler Youth

It was the fourth day after we had left Wiedersdorf. The atmosphere had changed a lot since we set out from Tabarz. Although the way was straight and easy now, and there was no gunfire to dodge, there was a different sort of menace in the air. Like the people we met in the towns and villages along the way, we too had become more suspicious and more self-reliant. In some ways we were happier keeping ourselves to ourselves and not falsely hoping for a good meal and a warm bed at the end of each day.

As we walked on we fell into the company of two

boys, Claus and Wolfgang. Much of what I know about their story and this part of the trek comes from the many reminiscences I had with Eva in later years. But I do clearly remember the first time we saw them. They were wearing shirts that were several sizes too big and when they flapped open we caught sight of the distinctive brown uniform of the Hitler Youth. They were starving, so we gave them some of the American breakfast packs, which they devoured ravenously as we walked. They were both heading for Halberstadt, which was on our route. At first they were reluctant to talk, but Dr Hagen, accustomed from his teaching years to talking easily to lads, soon had them telling their stories.

'I've just turned sixteen,' Claus said proudly. 'My birthday is 20 April, the same as the Führer.'

We all had to celebrate Hitler's birthday, even little children like me, so we knew the date.

'And what've you been up to?' asked Dr Hagen. 'How come you're so far from home?'

'We've been fighting,' said Claus. 'With the Hitler Youth, helping to defend Magdeburg. It was pretty hairy, I can tell you.'

'You too, Wolfgang? Were you fighting too? How old are you?'

Wolfgang nodded before replying, 'Sixteen.'

I thought to myself that these boys were about the same age as my cousin Ulrich and, as far as I was concerned, Ulrich was not a grown-up. He was a big kid, who used to lead us into mischief at the brick factory house. Yet these two boys had been fighting a war. I can still picture Claus: he was quite small for his age and he had freckles on his nose. Wolfgang was slightly older and seemed a lot more mature, even in my eyes. He had cropped fair hair and blue eyes, and was taller than his companion. Neither of them had a voice that had broken, which made the reality of them fighting with guns and seeing their friends killed in front of them all the more poignant.

I know now that from 1942 onwards all boys over sixteen were called up to attend military training camps, a hard grind compared with their years in the Hitler Youth, which up to then had been like Scout camps with a heavy overlay of Nazi propaganda. But at the military camps they were put through intensive training to become soldiers.

The propaganda was unrelenting and they had classroom lessons with titles like 'Why We Are Fighting'. They were given phrases to learn, which included things like 'Let me take them all on! I will prevail because I know how to believe and how to fight.'

It was real brainwashing, so it is no surprise that these very young boys were often the last to surrender and found it harder than older soldiers to accept defeat. Boys of this age had been in the Hitler Youth, compulsorily, since they were ten and they had grown up almost all their lives in Nazi Germany, with its constant subtle drip of propaganda. Under certain circumstances it is easy to indoctrinate anybody, especially the young, who have no other experience of life and nothing to make comparisons with. By the end of the war, in cities like Berlin and Munich, boys as young as ten and eleven were pressed into service, dressed in uniforms that were too big for them and carrying weapons they did not know how to fire. For those recruited in the last mad days of the war, life expectancy was less than a month. Their combination of fanaticism and youthful recklessness meant many of these boys died in futile attempts to defend a defeated Germany.

Claus was a prime example of this kind of brainwashing, with what to us seemed overblown patriotism. As he walked along, he sang Hitler Youth songs, including one about how 'the flag means more than death', until Eva asked him to stop.

'It's not particularly wise, seeing there are American military convoys along this road, don't you think?' she asked drily.

'I don't care,' proclaimed Claus. 'I would have preferred to die in battle than to live under the Allies. We all know what's going to happen now. The German people are going to be made into slaves to the enemies. We'll be no better than animals.'

I looked at Eva, frightened, but she instantly reassured me. 'Now, you know that's not true, Claus. You're scaring Bärbel with your nonsense. All your so-called enemies have been very kind and friendly. They've been nothing but good to us.'

'Huh,' Claus answered scornfully. 'You don't know anything. You haven't been fighting them like we have.'

There was a lot of bravado to what he said, in his

piping, unbroken voice. Deep down, he was probably as relieved as the rest of us that it was over, but he found it hard to say so.

The other boy, Wolfgang, was more thoughtful, quieter and altogether more solemn. He perked up when Dr Hagen said that he did not believe that the occupation of Germany by the Allies would be oppressive.

'Will I be allowed to go back to school?' he wanted to know. 'Because I plan to train as an engineer, like my father.'

'I'm sure you will,' replied the doctor. 'This country is going to need as many qualified people as possible to help rebuild it.'

This seemed to lighten Wolfgang's mood and reassure him. He too was desperate for life to get back to normal; to reclaim his youth.

'Tell us about the fighting you were involved in,' said Eva.

As we walked, their stories gradually emerged.

It was just over a week earlier that Magdeburg had come under fierce attack from the Americans, with 300 planes dropping bombs on the city and intense artillery fire across the River Elbe. To defend the city, 800 boys from the Hitler Youth had been drafted in to join the other troops, with the idea of holding up the American advance on Berlin, which is what the German High Command assumed the Americans were doing. I read later that Magdeburg was where the Americans sustained their last casualty of the war, when one of their tanks was hit and the gunner killed. The German weapon that killed him, an anti-tank gun, was apparently fired by a woman, which shows how fiercely dedicated some people were to the cause.

Claus and Wolfgang were deployed in foxholes, usually rooms in damaged buildings or crude fortifications they made themselves from all the rubble and wood around them. They were in the outer suburbs, with a remit to defy and delay the enemy, and they became part of the final stand in which every block and every street in Magdeburg was fought over bitterly. They had weapons, but most of them were old relics of the First World War and not what the boys had been taught to use. They were forced to retreat further and further into the city, but then the Elbe bridges at Magdeburg were blown up, trapping them in the direct line of the advancing Americans. As the Germans were still bombarding the Americans from the other side of the river, their unit, and many others, were now under fire from their own side. They saw boys from their own unit killed. Eventually they were told by their commanding officer, who himself was only eighteen, to surrender and they did, although Claus insisted he would have preferred to die killing Americans.

They were taken prisoner by the Americans and questioned by a US sergeant, who seemed astonished when he saw that it was just young lads who had been fighting so fiercely. 'How old are you boys?' he asked and, when they told him he surprisingly switched to German and said, 'Get rid of those uniforms and get yourselves home, kids. Get back to your mothers where you belong.'

The sergeant was shocked. He did not believe in taking children as prisoners, so had let them go. Claus and Wolfgang were lucky. If they had managed to cross the river before the bridges were blown, they would have ended up in the hands of the Russians and it is unlikely that they would have had such a generous reaction from the Soviet forces.

Many of the Hitler Youth boys were from Magdeburg and some made their way back to their homes easily. Others, including these two, found bombed-out houses to shelter in, where they lived on the remains of their rations, and food that they scavenged and begged. When Claus and Wolfgang thought it was safe to set out for home, they knocked on the door of a house and asked if the people could give them any spare clothes, which is how they came to be wearing their oversized shirts. Then they set off.

Some of their friends, they told us, lived in the part of Magdeburg taken by the Russians and had no idea how they were going to get across the river to their homes, or whether it would be sensible to attempt it. They had left them in the ruins, living by their wits.

It was a terrible story. These two boys had seen truly awful things. It seemed to encapsulate the madness that had engulfed our country, that finally children were being asked to sacrifice their lives so pointlessly. But Claus and Wolfgang had survived, against the odds, and hoped to see their families again.

Claus was one of a large family and he told us how ashamed he was of his grandmother, a staunch Catholic, who always said things critical of Hitler and his regime. 'We had to pretend she was a little bit doolally,' he said, 'to stop us all getting into trouble.' His father and two older brothers were away fighting, and his mother was struggling to keep their small farm going, and look after his six little brothers and sisters. 'That's the only reason I'm glad to have survived, so that I can take a lot of the work from her shoulders,' he said.

Wolfgang was the oldest of three children. He said he was really grateful that the other two were girls, because even if the war had continued they would not have been called up. Both of them had been sent away from home as part of the *Kinderlandverschickung*, the evacuation of children to the countryside. (I read years later that, by order of Hitler, the word 'evacuation' was never permitted, because that was what the British called it. In Germany we called it the 'despatch to the country-side'.) Wolfgang had no idea where his sisters were, but the youngest was only ten, so Eva asked for her full name to see if she had been at the home in

Tabarz. Unfortunately she didn't recognise it but she did her best to reassure Wolfgang that his sisters were probably safe.

Before he was called up, Wolfgang had been at high school, hoping to do well and go to university. Wolfgang's father, like my father, had not been called up until the end of the war as he was also older and, as an engineer, did an important job. But eventually he got his call-up papers and a few months later Wolfgang too was sent to fight. He was very worried about his mother, as she had been left alone when they all went and from what he said it did not sound as though she was too good at coping. We could tell that he was desperate to get back to her and I knew exactly how he felt.

He was luckier than us, I thought at the time, because he did not have so far to go to get back to his Mutti. But when I reflect on it those boys, and all the others of their generation, were incredibly unlucky. I had had to confront the realities of war, walking through battlefields and smelling the rotting flesh of dead bodies. But they had been forced to take part, to kill others and to take pride in it. They were all forced to sacrifice their childhoods.

Claus told us that he was sure he had shot at least two Americans. Wolfgang made no such boasts. If he did have such horrific stories inside him, that's where he kept them.

Years later, when we discussed the boys, wondering whatever became of them, Eva told me that it was Wolfgang she worried about. 'Claus would be fine. He would get a job where he had to obey orders, or he would work on the farm, and he would never think too deeply about what he saw or what he did. Wolfgang was different. I only hope he did not spend the rest of his life tortured by the things he witnessed and the actions he was forced to take. They were only children,' she said.

It was just one day that we spent with the boys but I recall them vividly. I can clearly remember Claus pushing me in the pram, running for a little way and then giving it a huge shove, so that I sped away down the road, which was downhill. Eva shouted at him and he ran after the pram, laughing, and caught me. Luckily, because I was heavy enough, he had not been able to send me off too fast. It was hard to believe that this same boy, larking around with my pram, had, a week earlier, been killing soldiers, narrowly escaping death himself. Too young to shave, too young to vote, but old enough to die for his country.

————————

The road we were following was good, but hilly as we were passing through the foothills of the Hartz mountains. We saw the historic city of Quedlinburg, its tallest buildings rising above us on promontories. We avoided its centre, mainly to keep moving but also because we were unsure where there was trouble.

As we skirted round it, Dr Hagen was able to tell us about the town. He really did seem to know everything. Wolfgang and I listened attentively, but Claus was easily distracted. If American convoys drove past, we had to restrain him from shouting abuse at them. Eva reminded him that it was not too late for him to be taken prisoner. Wolfgang always pulled his oversized white shirt tighter to himself, making sure he obscured the uniform underneath, but Claus didn't bother.

Near Halberstadt we parted company. Claus and Wolfgang recognised where they were and we could see they were both excited to be close to home.

They could hardly bear to hang around long enough to say goodbye before they dashed off.

After they had gone Eva said, 'I just hope they don't have the same disappointment we had at Wiedersdorf.'

Halberstadt had been bombed – its cathedral was badly damaged – but we hoped that both their families were safe. For the nights to come, we included them in our prayers.

———

That night we slept in a very exciting place. In the dark it was dangerous to be on the road, partly because of the military traffic that lumbered along, and partly because Dr Hagen and Eva didn't trust some of the other refugees also on the road. It was at night that those who were hiding from the Americans travelled, mainly soldiers who had escaped capture and were trying to make it back to their families, but also the foreign workers who had been brought into Germany to work on farms and in factories, and who had freed themselves and were roaming the countryside, stealing alcohol and looting.

So when evening began to fall, we went into the woods at the side of the road, following a well-worn track. We intended to find a suitable place to shelter among the trees, as we clearly would have to sleep in the open. We left the track and after a short walk came into a clearing; there in front of us was a hide, a wooden house on stilts, which the foresters used. I knew what it was at once because I had been in a hide on the Sundermanns' estate in the Wartegau, which was used by hunters.

I was thrilled to see the hide. It looked like a treetop Hansel and Gretel house to me, a small wooden structure above the ground, with a crude ladder, just notches in a plank of wood. Eva was worried about my climbing up, but I was nimbler than either she or Dr Hagen and reached the top very easily. We had to leave the pram below, but we made sure we brought all our belongings up.

This hide might have been designed for watching wildlife because there were holes to look through and one of them was just above the floor level, as if meant for a child who was sitting down. More likely, the foresters stayed there, because we found some food – just packets of dried fruit and nuts, but they tasted so good. There was also a bottle with some liquid in, which both Eva and Dr Hagen sniffed but decided against drinking. Fortunately, we had had a drink and a wash from a stream not long before.

We settled down for the night, but I was too excited to sleep. From the window I could see the clearing, which seemed to be a focal point for the forest animals. We saw deer and I particularly remember two large stags with antlers. There were rabbits and wild pigs. I felt very safe and secure, being above the ground, and in the twilight it was as if the animals were putting on a floorshow just for me. Eva kept telling me that I needed to sleep, as we would have another long walk the next day, but I was too thrilled by what I could see. Night fell, but there was a good moon and the cabaret changed – now there were badgers and foxes. When clouds blocked out the light I could hear rustling and catch the occasional glint of eyes down below. I must have fallen asleep eventually, but I know I was awake long after my two companions. As I had travelled in the pram for much of the day, they were bound to be more exhausted than me. But even as they slept I was happy and secure, wrapped in my blanket, listening to Dr Hagen's gentle snores and feeling the warmth of Eva's deep, peaceful breathing next to me.

When we woke the next day it was bright sunlight, the forest was alive with the sound of birdsong and there were more rabbits hopping around the clearing. Magically, there was a mother deer with her baby, a real Bambi, snuffling about in the mossy undergrowth. I watched them, transfixed, until a noise somewhere else in the forest startled them. The mother lifted her head, looked around as if she were sniffing the air, then bounded away, the little one following closely. I was so glad it had not all been a dream and I was reluctant to leave. I could have stayed for hours, watching the serene forest life. But I knew we had to go on.

14

Just the Two of Us Again

In these last few weeks of defeat and occupation
there was chronic disorder. A surging tide of dis-
placed people roamed the roads. There were freed
prisoners of war — liberated British, French and
American servicemen trying to find their way back
to their own armies — and many dispossessed families, mainly old people, women and children, with
small handcarts containing all their possessions,
trying to find somewhere they could call home.
Everyone carried parcels wrapped with string, suit-
cases, wicker hampers, or shopping bags; some had

blankets across their shoulders. There were also the slave workers, the foreigners, mainly from the Baltic states, who had been forced to work in Germany and who saw their liberation as a crude opportunity to abuse what was left of the country; to loot, vandalise and even rape.

Without Eva to guide me through my own memories, I cannot put an accurate chronology on all the things I saw at this time. Her diary was written, in pencil, whenever she had a quiet opportunity to herself. But there were not many spare moments on this second leg and her notes are very sparse. A great many events went unrecorded.

I remember the roads getting gradually more and more crowded with refugees, and Eva huddling me closer to her. She was now very reluctant to share even more than the briefest pleasantries with other travellers. We saw children on their own, older than me but not old enough to be independent; we saw the very old being pushed on makeshift carts; we saw occasional German soldiers, no longer in charge but hurrying, like the rest of us, to their own personal destinations.

There were some volunteer organisations already

helping people. Villagers and farmers along the way would leave pails of water out by their gates for us to drink from. Once, when I think we were at Braunschweig (Brunswick), we were lucky enough to come across a camp of American soldiers, and there were American Red Cross girls handing out coffee and doughnuts. The smell of doughnuts, sweet and fatty, lives with me still. The girls looked so healthy, not skinny as we were; they laughed and joked with the soldiers and, as usual, petted me. We greedily stuffed doughnuts into our bags for later, for ourselves and to share with the others we met who had even less food than we did.

One day we saw a small group of people standing by the side of the road, gaunt beyond belief and wearing striped uniforms. They hardly looked like people at all but more like walking skeletons. Their heads were shaved. One of them had his hands out for food, the others did not seem to have the energy to beg.

'Who are they?' I asked Eva. I had not realised people could be so thin.

'I don't know,' she replied. 'I think they must have come from a hospital or something. They look so ill. They were probably being treated for their terrible condition somewhere that has now shut down.'

They were, of course, survivors of a concentration camp and I now realise they must have been among the healthiest of the survivors to have made their way from the camps to the road. We were to learn later of the appalling experiences of people in these camps and, together, Eva and I wept at the memory of those we saw and of how little we were able to do for them. Many years later, when I watched my own son dying from cancer and racked by chemotherapy, his hollow cheeks and gaunt frame reminded me for an instant of these men in their striped pyjama-like clothes, appealing to the world for help.

As a small child, I saw these poor scraps of humanity as just another enduring image of a world gone crazy, a world in which all order seemed to have been overturned and it was, truly, every man for himself. Now I look back with despair, wondering how people can treat others in this way. There are almost no words for the horror of it.

We saw other strange sights in the chaos that the

end of the war brought. Somewhere along our route we saw trainloads of human beings crammed into goods carriages, being taken who knows where. This must have been before we were in territory held by the Allies, but there was so much confusion, and such a welter of jumbled memories, that I don't know where it happened. Once, we saw a train stop and all the people were let out. They were some way from us and we watched them crawling like ants down the banks from the elevated train tracks, scrabbling down the steep embankments and scurrying away in all directions to make sure they were not captured again.

The talk on the road was always of where the Russians were. Everybody wanted to be with the Americans and the British, and we were all terrified of falling into the hands of the Soviet troops. We kept ourselves to ourselves and Eva cautioned me about being too free with information about where we were going. If asked, she would simply say, 'Hamburg.'

'Hamburg' had now become a name as loaded for me as 'Wiedersdorf' had been on the first leg of our long march. Hamburg was where we would find our mother and it really did sound like home, in a way that Wiedersdorf never had, because it would be our permanent base, just as it had been before the war. Naively, even though I knew that our home had been bombed, I dreamed of it being rebuilt exactly the same and of us running into the big wide hallway to find Mutti waiting for us, with delicious smells coming from the kitchen and a big bowl of gooseberries for me to prepare. As we walked, we endlessly reminisced about the Hamburg we had known and loved before the war.

'You mustn't be disappointed if it's not the same as before,' cautioned Eva when she saw me getting carried away. 'It will be very different now.'

But she was never downbeat, never depressed. She told me it was a good thing that we had not met Mutti in Wiedersdorf and then been stranded there.

'Omi and Opa would not have been able to do this walk,' she said. 'Thank goodness they all managed to get home on a train. Little Henning would not have been able to walk, either, and the pram would not support both of you.'

She did not know how right she was. If we had

all stayed in Wiedersdorf for a couple of months longer, we would have ended up in East Germany, the Russian-occupied territory.

———

We were nearing Celle, where our friend Dr Hagen would leave us. The three of us spent our last night together sleeping outside. We were not lucky enough to find another hide, but we did find a dry place in some woods. There were others camping nearby and they had made a fire, but we didn't join them, preferring to settle down with our blankets wrapped tight round us; some bushes sheltered us on one side and the pram, laid down on its side, was on the other.

Eva and Dr Hagen were aware of the risks from scavengers, so we put our few possessions between us and the doctor used a large hankie to tie the handle of the pram to his wrist, so that he would wake if anyone tried to move it. We really did not want to lose our precious pram and we knew that others on the road looked at it covetously. Some of them had nothing to carry their belongings in and staggered under the load of small children. Others had handcarts. But ours was a highly sprung, well-made piece of engineering, light to push, yet very sturdy. Many, many times we said our thanks to the American GI who had loped away with our heavy, unwieldy wheelbarrow and brought us this pram in exchange. Now, if anyone tried to steal it, it would wake Dr Hagen, who must have had a rather uncomfortable night tethered to it.

We had finished the last of our American army rations and were becoming increasingly hungry. We had some bread to eat that night, but there was nothing to have with it except water from a stream. I can remember my hunger keeping me awake for a while, my tummy rumbling noisily. But eventually I slept and we woke to another warm spring day.

We were up early, partly because our makeshift beds were so uncomfortable and partly because Dr Hagen was eager to be up and off now that we were so close to his home. After a short walk, we came into the ancient town of Celle and Dr Hagen left us at last. Before going, he gave me my last lesson. I had learned so much from him, almost as though I had been in a travelling schoolroom. His parting

gift to me was a potted history of Celle, in particular its connections with the composer J. S. Bach,
and he whistled airs from Bach's music to me.

Although Dr Hagen was undemonstrative and,
for the most part, taciturn (we had learned very
little about his private life), he had been a very good
companion to us. We were sad to part from him,
but of course we were happy for him that he had
reached home. Besides the security of having a man
with us, it had also been very good for my sister to
have an adult to talk to and seek advice from. While
they were chatting, I could sit in my pram, look
around, and dream of home and Mutti.

Only someone who has been forced apart from
their mother as a child will understand my longing
to see her. Eva was a wonderful substitute mother,
always putting me first and doing everything she
could to protect me from the realities of what we
were passing through. But all the same, I longed
for my own bed and Mutti telling me stories as she
plaited my hair. I constantly dreamed about her,
day and night. I dreamed I heard her laughing ahead
of us in some thick undergrowth that we were
hacking down to get to her; I dreamed so vividly

that I could smell her perfume and hear the rustle of her skirt.

But we were now very close to seeing our mother again. Eva showed me on the map, and we knew that we would probably have to spend only one more night on the road before we reached Harburg, the town which occupies the south banks of the Elbe directly across from Hamburg on the north.

I was beginning to get excited again. We had been on the road for six days, but the long trek was going to be worthwhile, because in two days' time we would be with our family again.

We set out jauntily. The roads were clearer and we were once again walking on our own for most of the time. We sang, because our spirits were high. We ate more bread and we still had some of the American Wrigley's chewing gum, although I'm not convinced it helped with the hunger pangs. It seemed to make my tummy rumble even more.

The lush, pine-wooded countryside was giving way to a much flatter but equally spectacular terrain, the Lüneburg Heath. This is a huge, 200-square-kilometre stretch of mainly uncultivated land, with odd small-holdings dotted about and with its own peculiar brand of sheep, the *Heidschnucken*, who look as though they are half goat. Shepherds to this day still wear traditional green smocks. The heath is a mass of heather and in the summer it bursts into deep purple colours, edged with the bright blue bell flowers, which grow in profusion. At the time we were passing through, its colours were more subtle greens and greys. (I would see it in full bloom in the not too distant future, in more settled times.) The landscape was created in medieval days, when forests were cleared for the firewood, which was used to distil salt, the main industry in the area. Today the area is famous for its beauty and for its preservation of an old way of life: cars are prohibited in many areas, so horse-drawn vehicles and bicycles are the most common forms of transport.

We saw hawks hovering in the air before swooping to prey on small field animals and I learned to recognise the harsh chatter of jays, which sounded as though they were always in a bad temper and scolding someone, and the caw-cawing of the flocks of crows that assembled on the gnarled oak trees. I discovered that in the hedgerows were thin strips of tin foil, blackened on one side, and I

lucky enough to come across a woman in the garden of one of the cottages who gave us drinks of milk and some bread and honey. She was rather brusque, complaining about the number of refugees and how she could not be expected to feed them all. But as we were the first of the day, she said, she would make an exception for us. Even though her words were sharp, her voice was not aggressive and when she saw me she said, 'Poor little one, you need something to eat.'

The honey from the Lüneburg Heath is a famous delicacy and most of the small farms have their own hives to collect it from bees who feast on the heather during the summer months. It has a warm, heathery taste to it and on fresh bread it made one of the best breakfasts I have ever eaten – although that was probably because I was so hungry.

It was now 29 April, twenty-two days since we'd left Tabarz and, unbeknown to me, momentous events were happening. This was the day that Hitler, preparing for death, married his mistress Eva Braun. The following day they would commit suicide together in his bunker in Berlin, along with members of his High Command. Eight Russian armies were surrounding the capital city and even the most diehard Nazis were facing up to the reality of complete defeat. Five days after this the Lüneburg Heath would gain its own place in history, as it was here, on 4 May 1945, that the British military leader Field Marshal Montgomery received the unconditional surrender of all German troops west of the Elbe, including those in Denmark and Holland, three days before the final end to the war when Germany conceded defeat on all fronts.

We were now in the British-held area of Germany and, as we walked, we no longer met American soldiers. For the first time we met the British army. The uniforms were different, but to me the soldiers were all the same: friendly men with smiling faces who gave us food from their ration packs and spoke politely to my sister whose fractured English seemed to amuse them. Occasionally one of them wolf-whistled at Eva, but they all behaved with respect and kindness, just as we had come to expect from the Americans. The British were not as chatty as the Americans, or as ready to tell us their names (although that was not unusual to us, as Germans are rather formal) but they were just as generous and we liked them just as much. We got more corned beef, which we devoured gratefully. I ate so much corned beef at this time that today I cannot face it, except to cook it in a corned beef hash. The thought of the yellow fat around it in the tin turns my stomach, but I am grateful that I can be so picky. Back then, a tin of corned beef was manna from heaven.

There was another, much darker, reason why this area gained a place in the history of the war and the whole history of what the Scottish poet Robert Burns two centuries earlier called 'man's inhumanity to man'. It was on the fringes of the heath, near the pretty village of Bergen, that one of the most notorious of all the concentration camps, Bergen Belsen, was established. We pushed our pram through Bergen, with no idea that four miles away lay this graveyard for human bodies and souls, a place where unredeemable sins were committed: 50,000 people died there, many from starvation and disease, others because of the cruel decrees of the notorious camp commandant, Josef Kramer, known as the Beast of Belsen, and his lieutenant, Irma Grese. It was here that Anne Frank perished.

The camp was liberated by the British on 15 April, just two weeks before we passed through, and they discovered thousands of unburied corpses and mass graves containing an estimated 40,000 bodies piled into pits. Belsen was not an extermination camp: there were no gas chambers as there were at other terrible camps. But the imprisonment of so many men and women in such a small space with few provisions and inadequate sanitation meant disease was rampant and it contributed to Hitler's ultimate aim of extermination as effectively as any planned murder.

Even just the day before British soldiers walked into the camp, the guards opened fire on inmates who, having spotted the white sheets of surrender, had rejoiced at the approach of the Allies. The troops who arrived in tanks the next morning found 38,000 survivors but, tragically, most of them were so ravaged by disease and hunger that 28,000 of them died, despite the medical care that now came to them as fast as the British could get it there. The camp was in chaos when the troops arrived: order had completely broken down and there was no food except in a locked building crammed with

read and seen much about it since I moved to Britain, in books and on television. I have not shied away from it. I cannot apologise for what I, as a seven-year-old, knew nothing about. One of the criticisms levelled at my nation is that we must have known what was happening, we could not have coexisted with these horrendous camps without having some idea of what was going on inside them. This may, perhaps, be true of those who lived near them. But our metropolitan life in Hamburg during the early days of the war, our time in the Wartegau and our return to Hamburg when everything was over meant that my family, like millions of others, was genuinely insulated from these appalling excesses. I know now, although I was far too young to understand it, that there was racist propaganda, and my parents and sisters probably knew Jewish friends who fled before the war or who lost everything and simply disappeared. But we had, I swear, no idea of what they fled from. When I read about what happened, and when I read *The Diary of Anne Frank*, I cried the same tears as anyone would cry reading her story. For me, there was a peculiar resonance: Anne was slightly older than me, but she was a child of my time, living under a regime that I lived under, but with widely different results. I cried bitter tears, not only for Anne but for my guilt by association and for a country which, somehow, allowed an Austrian madman to take over and commit, in the name of Germany, such atrocities.

We walked on that bright spring morning, unaware of what had happened so close by. I can only be glad that we did not know then, as we had to keep up our spirits if we were to survive what lay ahead.

15

The Plunderers

There were more travellers on the road now, but we were still making very good speed. A lift on the back of a farmer's cart helped us, allowing Eva to rest her legs until we got beyond the town of Soltau. We walked on and it was getting towards time for us to have our lunch. We had our British rations, which was exciting for me because I had no idea what was inside the packs and was looking forward to discovering what they contained.

'I think we'll have to leave the road, Puppe,' said Eva. 'We need something to drink and there's nothing along here. If you spot a stream or building, we'll turn off and have a little picnic, all right?'

It sounded like a good idea to me and I would be glad of a drink. The streams and brooks, which had been so plentiful earlier in our walk, were now much more difficult to find.

A few hundred yards further on Eva noticed a farmhouse down a track. 'What do you think? Shall we go over and see what we can find?'

I agreed with Eva, as I always did. So we turned off the road and made our way down the track towards the building. As we approached it we could see it was deserted and falling into ruin, although the fields around it were cultivated.

'Oh, it's a ruin,' Eva said, disappointed. 'There won't be anyone there. Oh, well, let's carry on anyway. There might be a well or a tap that we can use.'

We carried on towards it and were almost at the outbuildings when across the green field a dark shadow seemed to emerge. As soon as we saw it we froze and watched, semi-paralysed, as it approached. The shape shifted and separated until it became clear. It was a band of men, about twenty-five of them, wearing rough, dark clothing and with dark hair and beards, a frightening gang of what we called 'plunderers', the freed slave labourers who were roaming the countryside scavenging and looting.

It took a couple of minutes for Eva to shake off her paralysis. Then she whispered urgently, 'Don't argue with them, don't disobey them, do exactly what they say and say your prayers.'

As she told me this, she deftly threw a few bits from our pram into a nearby ditch. I was transfixed and terrified, clutching Charlotte to my face but peering over her head at the approaching menace. We did not try to run or hide: there was nowhere to go, and they were moving at speed and had seen us.

As they got nearer my terror deepened. The men were oddly silent, just one or two of them barking what were probably orders in a guttural language that we could not identify. We knew it was not German, French or English. The whole group seemed to move as one, coming towards us through the field without swerving or splitting up.

Then they were upon us. I clutched Eva's hand tight. They were dirty, dressed in dark jackets and

ragged trousers. Some had boots, others were bare-
foot, with rags tied round their feet. They smelled
very strongly of alcohol. Some of them, probably
about half, were brandishing pistols. I closed my
eyes tight when they were a few steps away and fer-
vently prayed for them to move past us, to keep
going and leave us alone. But my prayer was not
answered, and they descended on us with strange
whoops and cries.

A few seemed to sheer off and start exploring the
farm buildings. I heard crashing noises, the shat-
tering of glass and the splintering of wood, as they
wrenched off doors and smashed windows, looking
for things to take. But the others surrounded us,
grabbing the stuff from our pram and thrusting it
into the sacks that most of them seemed to be carrying. They looked at us and one of them grabbed my
arm while three or four of the others pulled Eva away
from me, leering at her and cackling an uncouth
laughter that I can still hear. I screamed and the one
holding me clenched his fist and threatened me with
it.

As she was dragged away, Eva called, 'Remember
— do what they say!' Then she said 'Charlotte',

which was our code for me to cover my face with my doll. She must have been terrified, but she was still thinking of me.

They dragged her into a tumbledown wooden shed. The man holding me thrust me against a wall and gestured for me to sit down on the hard ground. I obeyed. I did not dare move, not even to turn my head to see what was happening. I kept my face buried in Charlotte shielding my eyes behind her blue velvet hood, now tatty and dirty from our travels, rigid with fear of what was happening to my sister.

The wild men seemed to ebb and flow around me, calling to each other as they swept rapidly in and out of the crumbling buildings. They ignored me, until one of them suddenly pounced on me, tore Charlotte from my hands and stuffed her into his ragged sack, jabbering at me in the language that meant nothing to me. I wanted to call out, protest and try to hold on to her, but I was too scared. I remembered what Eva said and knew I had to let the man take Charlotte away if he wanted to.

I can still picture the man who took Charlotte.

He had a pistol tucked into the top of his trousers, which were held up with string. His boots had no laces, his face was black with ingrained dirt and he had a mouth full of broken teeth; bushy black eyebrows met over his nose, and his chin and cheeks were covered with dark stubble. A black bandanna on his head made him look to me like every image of a bandit I had ever conjured up in my worst imaginings. He stank of alcohol and sour sweat.

I squeezed my eyes tight shut after he wrenched Charlotte away, convinced that he was taking her from my face so that he could shoot me more easily.

I sat motionless, holding my breath, my hands in my lap, feeling empty without Charlotte. I was so terrified I could not think of beautiful memories, which is what Eva had told me to do if ever I was frightened. When he did not shoot me, my biggest fear was that I would hear the sound of a gunshot from the shed. I could only think that they had taken Eva away to kill her: I knew of nothing else they could do to her. But, thank God, the sound never came.

After what seemed like an age, the men reassembled at some indefinable signal into their strange and awful band, and departed as suddenly as they had arrived, taking off across the fields once more, travelling fast, ignoring the track that led to the road, until they all merged into one again and became an ever smaller splodge of black on a green and grey landscape.

It was only when they had utterly vanished that I dared to move. My muscles were almost in spasm from being held so tight for so long. I stood up gingerly and looked about me. Our pram was still there, although it had been roughly thrown on to its side. There was nothing left in it.

I called Eva's name, but to my horror there was no reply. Slowly, because I was deeply afraid that one or more of the men had stayed behind, I went towards the shed where I had seen her taken. I was terrified of what I would find, imagining the corpse of my sister abandoned there. I had seen enough death to know what it looked like and to have no trouble visualising it.

As I went through the broken-down door into the shed I heard a sound. I was hugely relieved – Eva was not dead! But the noise was the sound of her sobbing, deep, racking sobs that must have shaken her whole body. I could not see her, stepping from the bright midday light of a fine, warm spring day into the darkness of the barn, but gradually my eyes adjusted and I could make out her shape. She was lying on a thin layer of straw with some old milk churns behind her.

'Eva,' I said timidly and this time she heard me, hurriedly turning and putting her clothes in order.

She quickly wiped her tears and sniffed, saying, 'Puppe, darling little Puppe, are you all right? Did they hurt you?'

I ran over and threw myself down in the straw with her, all my pent-up fears releasing themselves in tears of joy that we had both survived. Eva held me tight and for a long time we sobbed in each other's arms.

This was only the second time that Eva revealed her true emotions to me. The first had been when we discovered Mutti had left without us. At every other stage of our difficult journey she had been upbeat, always seeing the bright side of everything, relentlessly cheerful to keep my spirits high. But the horror of this attack was too much. Even Eva's spirit was broken by this outrage that had been committed against her and by the great fear for my safety that had engulfed her. We cried until we were both exhausted with the effort of heaving sobs out of our bodies. Then we lay quietly holding each other for some time.

When I remember this awful moment, I can still feel Eva's body trembling and hear her bitter weeping.

For days afterwards, whenever she thought I was not aware, tears would roll down her cheeks, and she would quickly and surreptitiously brush them away. At night, when she cuddled up to me, I would stir in my sleep and feel her thin body racked with silent sobs.

I knew nothing about rape until years later. Children were innocent in those days, and their innocence was prized and protected. I knew the men had been cruel to Eva: their sour smell — sweat, alcohol, tobacco, dirt — lingered on her as we lay in the hay. I realised her clothes had been torn, and when we finally sat up and took stock, it took her a few minutes to get dressed properly again.

We never talked about it. In years to come, when we discussed our walk from time to time, if I mentioned the 'plunderers' she would agree with me that they were very nasty men, but she would only talk about what they stole from us. She never mentioned the biggest theft of all: her virginity. In those far-off days, girls like us preserved ourselves for our husbands and for Eva what was taken from her that day, in such a cruel way, was a huge loss. I don't know any details, but she must have been raped by several of them, not just one. Reminded of it, her eyes would swim with tears and mine would, too. Today, as I write this, there are tears running down my cheeks, tears for her loss and for the dreadful ordeal she suffered, but also for her bravery, which I did not fully appreciate until years later.

She locked away what happened. She could not confide it to anyone, even to herself in her own private diary. She later wrote:

Then came the biggest disaster of the whole journey. We were stormed by twenty-five plunderers. When you see twenty-five wild men come running towards you, what can you do? You just have to shut up and endure whatever happens.

I know that some of her friends and our parents' friends back in Hamburg, girls of the same sort of age, also endured attacks and rapes by Russian soldiers, but none of them dwelt on it. Today we have a culture of therapy, everybody talking about their bad memories, but in those days we were preoccupied by survival and Eva was not alone in burying deep inside her the terrible wrongs she suffered in those minutes she endured in that dilapidated shed. Who is to say what is the best way of coping? My dear sister appeared to regain her normal self almost at once, but if the subject of the day ever came up, I could see the fear in her eyes.

On that day in April 1945 Eva was, as always, a pragmatist and as we sat in the hay she said to me, 'Well, Puppe, we are both alive and well. That's as much as we could ask, isn't it? We must thank God for that. He answered our prayers.' She got up from the hay stiffly and stretched.

'They took Charlotte,' I said.

'Oh, little one. That's terrible. But you mustn't worry because when we get home you will have more dolls.'

'I want Charlotte,' I said indignantly. Looking

back, I am ashamed of myself. What was my loss compared with hers? But I was too young to understand, and Charlotte had been a shield and companion for me through difficult and terrifying experiences. Now I wonder what made the plunderer take her and thrust her into his sack. She had no value. At best, she was a home-made rag doll, and by the time he seized her she was very battered and worn. I can only conclude that he did it purely out of spite, revenge, a need to make things as horrible as possible for us.

'Let's see if we can find that drink we wanted in the first place,' Eva said, quickly back to her old self.

We went outside and the first thing we did was to go to the ditch where Eva had thrown some of our things. The plunderers had missed them and we retrieved Mutti's Metwurst sausage, the watch the soldier had given Eva as a keepsake and her diary. I wished with all my heart that I had thrown Charlotte into the ditch with them. We had lost everything else, including Eva's own watch, and a ring had even been taken off her finger. But we knew we were lucky, because they could have shot us and nobody would ever have known who did it.

Our bodies might have lain there for weeks before being found. We also realised later that it was a good job our friend Dr Hagen was no longer with us as he would undoubtedly have been shot, and probably we as well because we would have been witnesses. Also, many years later, when I heard about the rape of small children, I realised that I was lucky to have gone untouched. All in all, with so many horrific things happening in those lawless days, we were very fortunate that it hadn't been worse. Neither of us could ever bear to think of what would have happened to me if they had killed Eva.

We righted the pram and Eva said cheerfully, 'Well, at least they didn't take this, so my little princess still has her carriage. And we will make such good progress now that we have nothing to carry apart from ourselves, won't we?'

We found a pump and Eva had a good wash, although we no longer had our beautiful soap and our soft towel, and we both finally had that much needed drink. But the plunderers had taken our dishes, so we had to hold the water in our cupped hands.

Then Eva said, 'We're so hungry, I don't think

Mutti would mind one little bit if we ate some of her sausage.'

So we ripped the Metwurst apart with our fingers, as we had no knife, and broke off lumps to eat. It was very unappetising, as it is meant to be sliced thin and eaten with bread, and we were chewing our way through mouthfuls of it, spicy and fatty and, to me, revolting.

When I pulled a face and spat some out, Eva coaxed me: 'We need food, Puppe. We must eat, to have the strength for the last little bit of our journey. Two days from now we'll be eating with Mutti, remember. We just have to be fit and strong to get there.'

So, reluctantly, I persevered, thinking longingly of the British army ration packs that had been stolen from us. I never found out what was in them, but I know it would have been easier to digest and altogether more appetising than chunks of fatty sausage.

As we ate, I slipped my hand into my trouser pocket and there was the little wooden train that I had secretly brought from Tabarz. I still didn't tell Eva I had it, as I felt naughty not obeying the instruction to bring only Charlotte. But I fingered its familiar shape and felt reassured: something of mine had survived the plunderers.

After we had rested a short while and gnawed at the sausage, we had another drink and set off again, following the track that had brought us from the road to the ruined farm where these 'horrible men', as I called them, had found us. Eva told me later that I used to say 'horrible men' and wrinkle my nose and turn down my mouth and shudder whenever I thought about the attack.

Eva, being the kindest, best sister in the world, immediately tried to distract me from my awful memories. She started singing and I quickly joined in. Then she asked me what story I would like to hear and I chose one of my favourite fairy tales. When the story was over we talked about our mother and father, and our cousins Volker and little Henning, and all the rest of our family who, she said, would be waiting to welcome us to Hamburg.

Without Eva's watch, we had no idea of the time. The watch the soldier had given her was not wound up, so had stopped. From the position of the sun we guessed it was still afternoon.

'If we press on,' said Eva, 'we will only need to spend one more night on the road.'

By late tomorrow we would be with our family.

16

So Close to Home

The road was clear and we made good progress. After a few miles, soon after Wintermoor, we were overtaken by a young woman of about Eva's age, who was going in the same direction. She asked very politely if we minded her walking with us, as she was frightened by the look of some of the people on the road. We knew well what she meant and were more than happy to let her accompany us.

Her name was Fraulein Gerda and she, like Eva, had been working as a teacher in one of the BDM homes. They had plenty to chat about and I was glad she was there to distract Eva for a while from the misery we had been through so recently. They talked nostalgically about their classes of girls, wondering whether they had all managed to escape back to their own homes. Gerda had taken a party of her girls back to Hanover, where they were from. Some had found their families, others had to be billeted with volunteers and she had been reluctant to leave them. She was worried about them, but she felt it was her duty to get home to her own mother and younger sister. They lived in Harburg, which was where we were heading before we went into Hamburg, so we agreed we would all stick together until we got there.

When we told Gerda how far we had come she was astonished, and very impressed that I had walked so far and that I was so uncomplaining. I remember feeling very proud. 'My girls only had to go twenty miles!' she said, looking at me with admiration. 'But some of them made a great fuss about it and they are four years older than you. What a very grown-up, brave girl you are.'

Gerda was a good companion and the miles

passed swiftly. It was on this stretch that the sole of one of Eva's sturdy shoes, which had done such good service, broke free from the uppers and flapped open. We had nothing to tie it up with, as everything we possessed – even our hankies – had been taken by the plunderers. So Gerda gave Eva one of her hankies and we ripped it into strips, tied two or three together and bound it round the shoe, like a bandage. Once again, we thanked God for the warm dry weather. If it had been raining or damp on the ground, Eva would have had one very wet foot. Now it looked as if it had been bandaged and I made the others laugh by asking Eva every so often, 'And how is your shoe doing? Is it getting better? Can we take the bandages off soon?'

By nightfall we were at a village called Steinbeck and we tried to find somewhere to stay for the night. At one house where we knocked on the door a woman gave us a plate full of boiled cabbage and potatoes, which was very welcome, but she could not offer us accommodation. She would not even allow us into the house to eat, but served us outside and watched us sharing the food, to make sure she got her plate and spoon back. She must have had some bad experiences with the travellers who were passing through.

We walked on and after a while we spotted a barn some way from a cluster of farm buildings. It was getting dark, so Eva and Gerda decided we would creep in and sleep there. As long as no dog was about to alert anyone in the farmhouse that we were there, we should be undisturbed for the night.

The barn turned out to be a stable block, with several horses in it. Each had its own stall, but there was an empty one with a plentiful supply of clean hay in it and we settled down very comfortably. The drawback was that we were so terribly hungry.

'Can I eat some hay?' I asked Eva. 'The horses seem to like it.'

'No,' said Eva, though she couldn't help laughing. 'It wouldn't be good for you at all.'

'It doesn't hurt the horses,' I countered.

'No, but you're a little girl, not a little horse. I know you're hungry, sweetheart, but try not to think about it. Remember – we'll be at home tomorrow and everything will be all right.'

We still had a bit of the horrible sausage to chew, which at least kept the worst of my hunger pangs at bay, but I longed for a proper meal with the delicious food that Mutti made for us.

It was nice settling down to sleep with the snorting of the horses and the occasional stamp of their feet, and the low whispering of Eva and Gerda, who were still chatting quietly. I slept well, much longer than the night before in the woods and without any disturbing images of plunderers invading my dreams.

Afterwards, Eva wrote in her diary:

we thought that this would be our last night, but things always work out differently from what we expect.

When we woke the next morning, we were surprised to see the rafters of the stables were full of bats, hanging upside down to sleep. I had seen bats, as there were plenty flitting around the brick factory as twilight fell, but I had never seen them at rest before. Eva and Gerda were both a little bit afraid of them and were really glad we had not seen them when we crept into the barn. I did not mind them too much, but I was worried about them hanging so precariously and I was sure they would have to drop when they relaxed. Eva explained that they would not fall, but we were all glad to say goodbye to the horses and creep out of the stables.

When we got outside, we were accosted by the farmer, who was on his way in to attend to the horses. He was as surprised to see us as we were to see him. He was not angry, though, especially as Eva and Gerda both apologised very politely, and assured him we had stolen nothing. He told us to go to the farmhouse and his wife would give us some milk. We were very grateful. She also gave us some bread and butter, and we borrowed a knife to slice thinly the remaining bit of the sausage. It was much more palatable eaten with bread and butter and a glass of milk.

Before we set off again, the farmer directed us to an outside wash-house and lavatory, which he said we could use. It was obviously provided for his farmworkers, but he had no workers left and was grumbling about how much he had to do himself. It was a big, well set-up farm, with fields of crops stretching into the distance. Inside the wash-house, which was little more than a wooden shed with a standpipe for washing, we found a three-seater toilet: it was a large hole, presumably over a cesspit, with three holes in the wooden board over it and thin partitions between each seat. When you sat there you could hear the people in the other two seats, but you could not see them. We were all still very keen to stick together, so Eva, Gerda and I lined up side by side on this communal toilet.

Then something very funny happened. One of them, and I don't know which one, passed wind rather noisily. I was surprised and a little shocked. I had been brought up to believe this was something polite girls never did in the presence of others. But before I could get over my shock, the other one did the same thing. (It must have been due to the boiled cabbage we had eaten the previous evening.)

'Wow, this is obviously what grown-ups do in toilets,' I thought to myself. 'It's OK to do it in here. It must be a very grown-up thing to do.'

So I tried and I tried and I tried, puffing out my cheeks until they were red, but I could not do it. It must be the only time in my life when I have desperately wanted to blow off, to prove that I was a big girl. I was so proud of what Gerda had said the day before about me being grown-up and felt this was another chance to prove it. Alas, I failed. I didn't tell the other two about my attempt and failure, but in retrospect I wish I had: it would surely have given them something to laugh about as we set off walking again.

The end of our journey was at last in sight. We found a new lightness in our step, buoyed up as we realised that we were almost, *almost* home.

Eva and Gerda took turns pushing me in the pram when I was too tired to walk and, with our desire to get there forcing us onwards, the miles were eaten up rapidly. We could soon see the outlines of Harburg on the horizon, which quickened our step even more. As Eva and Gerda chatted happily, I wondered what to do first when we all got home. I had no idea where 'home' would be, but I was thinking of Mutti and imagining the kind of place she would have for us. She was a wonderful homemaker: she had turned the brick factory house into a warm, welcoming place, so I was sure we would have somewhere comfortable and beautiful.

I missed my Charlotte, but I was confident Mutti could make me another doll, exactly the same. I was planning what colour clothes we would make for her, and I wanted her face and hair to be just as Charlotte's had been. My excitement consumed the last few miles very quickly.

Two years before the outbreak of the war, Harburg was officially joined with Hamburg into one city, but the two remained separate and always will, because the mighty River Elbe flows between them. As if to reinforce the boundary, the river splits into two channels, the north and south Elbe, and so, effectively, there are two rivers to cross to get from one to the other, with a substantial island in the middle. Although Hamburg is more than seventy miles inland from the estuary of the Elbe, the size of the river is such that it is a major port for seagoing shipping, and both channels of the river are wide, deep and have strong currents. The island in between Harburg and Hamburg is big enough to have a whole town, Wilhelmsburg, on it, which is where Uncle Hermann, Henning's father, came from.

As we reached the outskirts of Harburg we said

goodbye to Gerda. She was now on her way home as well, and we said merry farewells and wished each other the best. Although we had become good friends, we did not exchange addresses because we did not have one to give her. A lot of brief, transitory, but nonetheless good friendships were made in wartime. Besides, we were so excited that we were within hours of finding our mother that we could not think of much else.

We made our way through the streets, which were as damaged as any we had seen from the bombing, towards the river. It was only as we approached the bridges which, remarkably, were intact that we realised the crowd had thickened. We were being jostled and pulled along by a throng of people, and when we were a few hundred yards from the river bank, we saw lots of British soldiers.

'What's happening?' Eva asked a woman nearby, shuffling forward with us.

'The bridges are closed. The British are not letting us cross,' she said.

'What?' cried Eva, her face anxious. 'Not letting us cross? Wait here, Puppe, I'll find out what's happening.'

She pushed me in the pram to one side of the road and left me there while she struggled through to the soldiers. She spoke to them in her fractured English and they told her that the bridges would probably be open later on, but that they could not let everybody surge across at once for their own safety.

In fact, it was no wonder that the bridges were closed to civilians. Although the British army had been camped just south-east of Hamburg since 19 April, it wasn't until the 30th, the day we arrived at the bridges, that they had finally been given orders to cross the Elbe and take the city, and it wasn't until 1 May that their troops streamed through the streets of Hamburg. They had moved into Harburg only hours before we got there.

There had been great anxiety in Hamburg for the past few weeks. Hitler had ordered that every city, town and village should be defended to the last man, but it was clear that the writing was on the wall and that any defence would be met by ferocious attack from the Allies, causing more needless death and suffering for the people of a city that had already been ravaged by the bombing.

Hamburg had never been a Nazi stronghold. Like most big seaports, it was cosmopolitan, outward-looking and there had been a sophisticated anti-Hitler movement in the city, particularly among intelligent teenagers who resented the regimentation and having to obey the orders of the Hitler Youth. Their rebellion took the form of listening and dancing to jazz: jazz was proscribed because it originated among the blacks and, so Hitler believed, the Jews of America. Many of these youngsters were arrested by the Gestapo and sent to concentration camps, but the very fact that the city bred and sheltered them shows that there was not quite the same frenzied admiration for Hitler as in some other cities. Radio Hamburg was the first station to broadcast the news of Hitler's death, on 1 May, the day after his suicide. The broadcast toed the party line by saying that he 'died fighting at the head of his troops', but by this stage of the war most adults were cynical about this. They believed he had died, but not the nature of his death. Only the diehard Nazi believers accepted it.

Immediately prior to the British taking the city, everyone living there was issued with an extra supply of food: one 2lb loaf of bread, a small chunk of bacon, half a pound of smoked sausage. This was on top of their normal rations and they were advised to keep it for 'the emergency'. They feared this meant they were going to be under siege or even attacked, so there was enormous relief and celebration when it was announced on 1 May that '*Die Stadt Hamburg wird aufgegeben*'. It was to be a peaceful surrender.

At the bridge entrance we were shepherded into a large hangar, with open sides and a glass roof. I think it must have been a market hall before the war, or a storage space for all the goods brought on and off the large ships that docked there, before they were loaded into proper warehouses. There were lots of people in the hangar but it was not as crammed as the mine we had sheltered in. There was space for everyone, plenty of fresh air and, thankfully, we did not feel claustrophobic. Little family groups had pitched themselves in their own areas on the floor. Eva and I found quite a good spot, from which we could view whatever was happening at the entrance to the bridge, and parked the pram. We found a couple of wooden crates to sit on.

Looking around, I saw that most of the others were women and children, with a few elderly men. There were hardly any younger men. The first night we spent there was miserable because we had no blankets and the concrete floor was hard and cold. At least I could sit in the pram, but I was so much too big for it that my legs splayed over the end and if I stayed in it for too long I got pains at the backs of my knees. I could not lie down or get comfortable enough to sleep. If we lay together curled up on the floor, the cold seeped through and made us so stiff that it felt as if we had been paralysed.

Eva got through the night without sleep and I dozed a bit. We were sitting on the crates, which we pulled close together, and I leaned on her shoulder with her arm round me. It must have been awfully uncomfortable for her, but we were both buoyed up by being so close to the end of our journey. The following day a group of Red Cross volunteers came round with a large handcart, offering hot soup and blankets, and we were able to get a blanket each from them to wrap ourselves in. After the lovely weather we had had for the duration of our walk, it had now turned colder and was raining, but at

rhymes to keep the rhythm going. We all became very good at it. For quieter times, someone gave me some string, and Eva and I would play the cat's cradle game. She always said I was better at it than she was.

We played word games and 'I Spy', and anything we could think of to pass the time. Once the charity soup was gone, there was nothing to eat at all, apart from some radishes off the back of a lorry that was also waiting to cross the bridge. The driver gave some to us all, for which we were very grateful, as they were crisp and fresh in our mouths.

The next day, after we had endured another uncomfortable night, the British started opening the bridge for pedestrians but only in short bursts, no more than half an hour a time.

'Now we will definitely get across,' said Eva confidently and every time there was any sign of movement among the soldiers or near the bridge we joined the general surge forward to cross. But the bridge was opened for such short periods that we never got through and that night we had to settle down to sleep yet again, wrapped in our blankets, on the hard floor. At least, as Eva said, we did not need to worry about anybody stealing our possessions, as we had none.

We stayed in the hangar for eight whole days and nights. It was truly terrible to be able to look across the river at the bulk of Hamburg, but not be able to get there. We felt we could almost see Mutti, as if we could just reach out and touch her, yet there was this huge barrier between us. Eva and I sang a song we knew about a prince and a princess who lived on opposite sides of a big lake that was very deep. They loved each other very much, but could not get to each other. It summed up how we felt about not getting to Mutti.

> *Es waren zwei Königskinder*
> *Die hatten einander so lieb*
> *Sie konnten zusammen nicht kommen*
> *Denn das Wasser war viel zu tief.*

> (There were a prince and a princess
> Who loved each other very much
> But they could not meet up
> Because the water was too deep.)

Throughout this time, apart from occasional cups of soup or hot drinks, we had nothing except radishes and water. Radishes, radishes, radishes. I don't eat them nowadays, although when I see a beautiful bunch in the supermarket I am sometimes tempted. But whenever I do have them they repeat on me. I think they are trying to remind me that once upon a time they saved my life.

These were the days of the most acute hunger. Everyone was conserving their own pathetic rations, so there was nothing to share with us. The soldiers could not give out food: they had very little spare for refugees and if they gave to one person they would be besieged by hundreds. There was a constant gnawing in my belly, as though there were an animal inside trying to eat its way out. All Eva could do was try to distract me. When the Red Cross workers appeared, nobody rushed to get their supplies: it was almost as if everyone was too exhausted, too disappointed and too determined not to miss out if the bridge suddenly opened, or risk losing their good places in the hangar. The women patiently came round to us and, seeing how skinny I was, they sometimes gave me a double portion of soup.

At first, the hunger kept me awake, but after that I was so tired I slept anyway. There were no washing facilities, but there were some crude lavatories, which I suppose were normally used by the dock workers. I hated having to go to them. I was brought up never to sit down on any toilet seat except our own, in case I picked up germs, so I was used to hovering above the seat. But these toilets were very unpleasant, with so many people using them. Because I was eating so little, I did not need to go as often as normal, which was a blessing in disguise, I suppose.

One day Eva said, 'I really can't take much more of this. I'm going to try to get us to the front of the line so that we will definitely get across when they next open the bridge. Watch this.'

She took one of our blankets, stuffed it up inside her blouse and went up to the British soldiers who were guarding the bridge. Then she tried to say in English, 'I am expecting a baby.' But she didn't know the English word 'expecting' and the German is '*Ich bekomme ein Kind*'. Translating this literally, Eva said, in her heavily accented English, 'I become a child.'

The soldiers laughed. They didn't believe in her

improbably shaped belly at all and thought her English very funny. Unfortunately, giving them a laugh was not enough to secure preferential treatment.

Sometimes we would be approached by men who appeared in the hangar offering to take us over by small boat under cover of darkness. They wanted money to make the trip and we had none since our encounter with the plunderers. But even if we had, Eva said we would not have risked it. The British were shooting anything that moved on the water at night, as they were still afraid there would be more resistance, even though the war was over, all but the signing of the surrender. Not only that but the crossing would be dangerous because of the currents, although these men claimed to be very familiar with the river.

The British troops were not supposed to fraternise with the Germans, but the soldiers we spoke to were always courteous and helpful. I don't think they knew when the bridge would be opened, as the commands came from above, so they were not being difficult when they said they could not tell us. There was some fraternisation going on, that's for sure. We saw German girls in lovely, bright, thin summer dresses, laughing and flirting with the soldiers, sometimes walking along arm in arm with them. Some of the people in the hangar tut-tutted about it and said the girls ought to behave with more restraint. But I think they were just young people, from both sides of the war, who had suffered a great deal and were now enjoying a bit of light relief. It did no harm.

The longer we stayed there, the more our small 'refugee camp' developed its own routines. Some of the women were particularly good at entertaining us children, and there would be story groups for the little ones and perhaps someone would juggle with some stones, or do conjuring tricks to amuse us. Charades became a popular diversion, and I envied the women and children who seemed to have a natural ability for the acting involved.

There was no routine, though, to the bridge opening. It could be at any time and it rarely lasted for more than half an hour, so we all stayed on constant tenterhooks. The Germans are not good at queuing, so whenever it opened we all pushed forward impatiently, trying to be the ones who got across. The sentries controlled it well, so there was no riot or fighting, but if you didn't get through, there was nothing to do but to go back and wait again. This happened a few times, but we always went back to our same spot in the hangar: it was as if everybody, after the confusion of the first day or two, respected everybody else's claim to their bit of territory.

On the eighth day, without any notice as usual, the soldiers suddenly announced that the bridge was open. Scooping our blankets into the pram, we dashed forward with the rest. Surely, at last, our turn had come . . .

I had grown so accustomed to being turned away that I could hardly believe it when Eva and I were ushered forward, past the barrier we had been longing to cross for over a week, to find ourselves actually on the south bridge. We laughed with delight as we realised that we were at last standing above the great river that had divided us from everything we yearned for. We pushed our pram across cheerfully, finally getting nearer and nearer to Mutti, walking on the pavements, as a steady stream of traffic, military vehicles and lorries with supplies for the city, edged bumper-to-bumper along the road.

Looking over the parapet of the bridge, I could see the huge ships harboured at Hamburg. 'They are as big as apartment blocks!' I cried in surprise. I had never imagined that ships could be so vast.

'Oh, Puppe,' breathed Eva, looking ahead to the island that lay between us and the city of Hamburg itself. 'We're nearly home.'

But when we reached Wilhelmsburg, the town on the island between the south and north bridges, there was yet another disappointment. The north bridge was closed. We were despairing: would we have to wait another eight days? How could we bear it? We didn't even have the radish man to keep us supplied. We were shepherded into another hangar with yet more crowds all waiting to cross the north bridge.

'I'm so sorry,' Eva said to me, as gently as she could. 'We will probably not get home to Mutti tonight. But with luck, we'll cross the bridge tomorrow. And do you know what? I've had a brilliant idea. Uncle Hermann's relatives live here in

Wilhelmsburg and I think I remember the address. We will go and find them and I'm sure that they will give us a meal and somewhere to sleep.'

When she had established that we certainly would not be allowed to continue crossing the river that day, Eva decided we should definitely set out to the Villa Cohrs in Dratelnstrasse, where she remembered visiting Uncle Hermann's family. We asked directions from a local person and off we went.

We made our way through devastated streets to the address Eva remembered and as we walked along the road towards it we already knew the worst: the house had been partly demolished, with the upper storey completely gone, and there was nobody there.

But luck, once again, was with us. The family's neighbours were there, living in a cellar under their ruined apartment block. They told us that the family had escaped unhurt, but they did not know where they had gone. Then they invited us in and made us very welcome. Most large apartment blocks in Germany have big cellars, which are divided into rooms for each family, with locks on the door so that they can be used to store surplus furniture, bikes and so on. This couple had made their home in their cellar room and there were other people living in the other rooms. We were given some food, which we devoured gratefully, and were invited to lie down on their beds for a rest. We both slept for a couple of hours and woke as daylight began to wane.

We declined their offers to let us stay the night. They really had no room, with four of them crammed into a cellar. And besides, we wanted to get back to the north bridge, because we needed to be there when it was opened. We did not want to risk missing it.

We spent a night in the hangar by the north bridge, hopelessly expecting to have to wait for many more days before we could cross, just as we had before. But to our great delight we were ushered over the bridge without too much trouble that very day. Because our arrival had coincided with the British taking control of the city, it had taken ten days in all just to cross the River Elbe.

Now we were truly going home.

and even if Mutti was not living with her, Aunt Käte would know where she was. We turned right as we left the bridge and headed towards her home in Caspar Voght Strasse.

It took us about two and a half hours of walking through streets which, although the debris had been cleared from them, looked alien without houses and offices and shops edging them. They lacked all definition. Whole areas of the city were flat, all landmarks gone. Temporary shelters and homes had sprung up in many places, but some districts looked as though they had been abandoned completely, the landscape bleak and bare. Sometimes a street looked complete, until I realised it was only the façades of the buildings that stood with nothing left behind them, like a film set. In other streets the houses were only half demolished, and people were living in the ground floors and cellars, always risking the crash of unsupported masonry on themselves and their makeshift homes. Some of the smaller buildings looked as if their roofs had been clawed by giant trolls. There were unexpected craters we had to skirt round, some of them filled with water. Charred debris lay everywhere.

tattered and dirty clothes. We saw squads of men working on the ruins, starting the huge clearing-up process that would turn Hamburg into the modern, beautiful city that it is today. We saw washing lines stretched across bomb sites, white towels and nappies fluttering in the spring breeze, reminding us of all the makeshift white 'surrender' flags we had seen draped from the windows in the towns and villages we had walked through.

The sights, sounds and smells of the city were plenty of distraction for us as we walked, and our pent-up excitement kept us going. We had had two cruel disappointments before: one short, sharp one at Wiedersdorf, and another drawn-out, daily, tor-turous one at the bridges, as every day turned into another long wait. But now, although Eva was trying to calm me down and prepare me for more delays, neither of us could think of any reason why we would not be with Mutti very, very soon.

As we neared Aunt Käte's street, our hearts were pounding. Eva clasped my hand tightly, as if to for-tify me against yet another disappointment. We had suffered so much in our long march to reach our mother. We needed to see her so badly that it was a physical ache. We'd hoped so much so many times before, surely now we wouldn't be let down . . .

'Come on, Puppe,' said Eva, her hand trembling slightly, as we turned into the street and began to walk down it. The road was untouched by the bombing, the small, neat bungalows intact. Which one was Aunt Käte's? Yes, things felt familiar; now we remembered. We could see her house. It was getting closer and closer.

Then, as we approached, I caught a glimpse of two heads and two backs bent low. Two women were crouching in the garden weeding. And I recognised both of them immediately, especially the beautiful curls of the woman on the left. It was my Mutti. At last I could see her.

Excitement and longing coursed through me. I pulled free of Eva's grasp and started running. I ran as fast as my tired, skinny little legs could carry me, my sore feet slapping on the pavement as I went.

'Mutti! Mutti!' I cried, breathless and panting, my heart pounding.

Slowly, she raised her head and looked up. For a moment she hesitated and frowned, as if she could not believe what she was seeing and thought it must be some mistake. Then, as joyful astonishment covered her face, she sprang up and ran towards us shouting, 'My Bärbel! Oh, my Eva!'

I bolted across the garden to her, crushing rows of asparagus as I flung myself straight into her open arms. Eva, finally able to abandon the pram, ran right behind me.

There are no words to describe the next few moments. The feeling of being close again to my mother was something I can never forget. She kissed my head and face as she wept and laughed in turn.

'My little girls! My babies. You're home. Thank God,' she cried, welcoming Eva into her arms as well. Both of us were laughing and crying, hugging her and refusing to let go until we remembered Aunt Käte, broke off to hug her too and then returned to Mutti's trembling arms.

Eva wrote in her diary:

The joy of seeing each other was huge. After we had talked and talked and cuddled and kissed and talked and talked and eaten we just all

fell asleep. I don't know how long
we slept, but it was lovely.

At last we were home.

For Mutti, the last few weeks had been agonising, with no news from us or from my father. She had already lost Ruth and now she didn't know whether she would ever see the rest of her family again. For her, the loss of one daughter had been insufferable and had made her very ill; I don't know how she would have coped if she had lost both of us, too. She had been trying to prepare herself for never seeing us again, so when she heard me calling her she couldn't believe at first that she was hearing correctly. But when she saw my fair head bobbing at speed across the garden, her relief and joy were immeasurable.

The decision to leave Wiedersdorf for Hamburg had been very difficult for Mutti. The others, our grandparents, Aunt Irma, Aunt Hilda, Volker and Henning, were going because they wanted to get back to the city before it was occupied by the British. They were afraid that after it was invaded they

might not be allowed in, and after our experience
with the long walk and the interminable waiting at
the bridges we could see it would have been very
difficult for them, particularly my elderly grandparents. So, after much agonising, Mutti had
decided to go with them, while there was still a
train to travel on. Her decision had cost her many
sleepless nights, when she lay awake terrified that
we had fallen into the hands of the enemy.

Later, when we gave Mutti and Aunt Käte a brief
history of our adventures. They listened with tears
running down their faces and they could not stop
hugging and touching us.

Aunt Käte's bungalow was small and she had her
own two children, Anne, who was Eva's age, and
Hansi, who was about sixteen, back at home, both
safely returned from their war work. Her husband
was still away. So the three of us shared one room,
with Mutti and me sleeping in the bed together and
Eva on a fold-up bed. Mutti told me later that
throughout that first night she kept waking and
looking at us, cuddling me gently so that she didn't
wake me, but satisfying her own need to hold me
and reassure herself that it was not a dream.

We slept very late, until the following afternoon, enjoying the most peaceful sleep we'd had since Tabarz. When we woke, Mutti and Aunt Käte had a hot bath ready. They plopped me in and scrubbed and scrubbed at me until I thought they were going to take my skin off. We hadn't had a proper wash for ten days, so I'm sure I was smelly and filthy, but nobody cared when we were reunited. I was not even in trouble for trampling the asparagus patch, which normally would have been a real crime, as it takes such a long time to establish.

They were going to throw all my torn and dirty clothes away, but I made a dive for my trousers and produced from my pocket the little train, wrapped in a tiny child's hankie: my souvenir, which I felt so guilty about. When I confessed to Eva about the train, she laughed and laughed. 'You could have told me, it didn't matter. I would have let you bring it,' she said.

So all my careful secrecy had not been necessary. But if I had been carrying the train and hankie in my little pink rucksack, they would have gone with the plunderers too, as my Charlotte did. So it was just as well I kept them to myself. I have them now, among my dearest possessions.

On that first day safe in Hamburg, reunited with our mother, Eva wrote in her diary:

> From 7 April to 18 May, many beautiful but also horrifying hours lie behind us. We have to thank God that we got out of it alive and that we are still in one piece.

For both of us, there was a tremendous sense of achievement. Eva showed me a map of what we had done and I ran my finger along the route. I have looked at it again many times, especially recently, as I have been writing this book. And I am filled now with the same amazement and pride I felt then.

WE HAD DONE IT!

18

Hammer Park

We lived with Aunt Käte's family for a month. It was a tight squeeze, but we managed well enough. Every house had to have a piece of paper pinned to the door stating how many people lived there, I think so that the British troops could identify places that were under-occupied. Aunt Käte didn't have that problem and now she had two more.

Power and water supplies for the city were erratic, but we were lucky because Aunt Käte lived near the two high schools (which I would later attend) currently being used as military hospitals, so every effort was made to keep on the supplies in that area. When there was no water we had to walk to standpipes, clanking our big metal buckets and hauling them back twice as heavy with the load – it would have been much easier with lightweight plastic ones, but unfortunately in those days there weren't any. I had to concentrate very hard so that I didn't spill much on the way home.

Then we had some great good fortune. Father had worked for the railways before he was called up and Mutti heard of a number of prefabricated houses (prefabs) that were being erected especially for the families of railway workers in Hammer Park, a beautiful place that was being used as a camp for British soldiers. She applied for a house and, probably because Father had a senior position, we were allocated one straight away. She rang and was told she could have number 43 Fahrenkamp, and we could move in immediately, although it was not finished.

There were several rows of these little cottages in the park, made somewhere in Scandinavia and assembled on site. There were similar emergency housing schemes in England, also put up in big cities to accommodate all the people who had lost their homes through bombing, or who were returning from the war and starting new families. Our new prefab was at the end of the row, so it was semi-detached, which gave us more garden than the others. When we moved in there were no windows, it was undecorated, the floor was concrete and, of course, we had no furniture. Even so, it felt wonderful to be able to close our own front door and be together again, just our little family of Mutti, Eva and me.

There had been no word from my father and we had no idea where he was, or even if he was still alive. Prisoners of war were beginning to arrive back, and we knew a few families who held celebrations when fathers and sons had been reunited with their loved ones. We clung to our prayers that we would be as fortunate, but as time went on our hopes diminished. We had to be realistic. Many families would never see their fathers and sons again, or even know what had happened to them, and there was every chance that we would be one of them. I was probably the least affected: I missed my father, but I had not seen him for so long, and I was so young when he left, that my life seemed complete as long as I had Mutti and Eva.

Within days of our moving in, the workmen on the site put in windows for us. Then we collected furniture from relatives who had escaped the bombing. Mutti had cousins who lived on the outskirts of Hamburg and whose houses had survived intact, and they all rallied round to give us things. One cousin of hers ran a well-established plant nursery and he presented us with fruit trees and bushes. We had a ceremonial planting to celebrate our new home: quince, cherry, apple, plum and pear trees, and redcurrant, blackcurrant and gooseberry bushes all had a place in our garden.

Sometimes I dream I am back in Germany, and I am usually in that garden, tending to the fruit bushes.

We loved that little house and we lived there for many years. It was on one floor and it had two bedrooms, a living room with a dining corner, a kitchenette and a cloakroom. There was no bath or shower, but we all grew used to having strip washes, and there were always friends and family who would let us have baths at their homes. We were so

Only now can I appreciate how desperate the times were. In some areas of the big cities, people were living rough, existing like troglodytes under the ruins of their homes. Food was so scarce that pet dogs were killed for meat, and stray cats were caught and cooked. We had a garden to grow things in and a proper shelter. We were very lucky.

The general shortage meant that treats were very rare and especially prized. One day, when we were staying with Aunt Käte, she asked me to help her bake a cake for her birthday. It was the first time in what seemed like a whole lifetime that I had done anything like that, although in fact it was less than six months earlier that I had baked Christmas biscuits with Volker and little Henning at the brick factory house. I loved helping Aunt Käte and I was allowed to lick the bowl. Then I had to go to bed, but I woke up the next morning, tremendously excited when I remembered the cake, and looked forward to my slice of it. To my great disappointment, the grown-ups had eaten the lot the night before. I think they had had a bottle of wine and were enjoying the occasion, and they simply forgot about me. I was so upset. It's funny how these griev-

said 'How nice to meet you' because we knew that if it had not been for the terrible war we would never have met. But it *was* nice to meet them — it was one of the good things that came from the war.

In return, I taught one or two of them German. They all wanted to know a few phrases, but a couple of the more serious ones learned to speak the language well and liked to practise with us.

Like all the soldiers we met on our travels, they grew nostalgic for their own children when they saw me and the other little ones. They produced photographs and told me about children who looked very like us, but who had strange-sounding names. I loved playing games with my friends, but I was also happy to sit and chat with the soldiers for long spells, so I became one of their favourites, their mascot. And their endless generosity continued as still they gave me food from their rations, which I always took home to the family. Food in general — especially luxuries — was scarce: we had tea bags from the soldiers, which we used so often that the water eventually ran clear. Mutti always dried them out, because she said that made them strong again. When, occasionally, Mutti had the ingredients to bake cakes, I would always take some to the soldiers, who really appreciated it as it was such a change from their standard-issue food.

There is one story I feel very guilty about and it still makes the colour rise in my cheeks to this day. One hot summer's day a small gang of us, boys and girls, came across a British soldier lying in the grass. He was fast asleep, snoring away, and he had taken off his belt and boots. The boots were so shiny and sturdy, and it was impossible to get hold of shoes at that time, so it was too much of a temptation and some of the boys stole them. I have worried about the soldier ever since: he would have had to go back to camp and explain that he had lost his boots and I'm sure he would have been in trouble. I would like to apologise to him, because although I didn't steal them, I know who did. My skin prickles with shame, even sixty years on. If he is still alive and reads this, I would like to make it up to him.

There was no school for us to go to. The schools that had not been razed to the ground had been taken over as military hospitals and, besides, it took many months to organise teaching staff and rewrite all the textbooks so that they were free of Nazi

the little boy died. Her father put his body in a cardboard box and set out on the long walk to the cemetery at Ohlsdorf, but unfortunately he didn't make it before the 6 p.m. curfew. Anyone found on the streets after the curfew was rounded up by the British soldiers and shepherded into halls and air raid shelters until the next morning. Karla's father spoke no English, but he knew the word for 'baby' was much the same in both languages – he had picked this up when two soldiers came to his house to check the number of people living there and heard them say 'little baby' about his son. So he approached the sentries and told them he had his baby in the box, but they didn't understand him and probably thought he was a bit crazy. He sat through that terrible night, clutching a box containing his dead son, and although he was with a crowd of people, he spent those hours bitterly alone in his overwhelming grief. The next morning, he walked on to the cemetery and handed the baby in to the mortuary. At home, his wife and daughter Karla stayed up all night, anxiously waiting for news of him and mourning the death of the baby boy.

Karla and I often played together, in our gardens

and sometimes exploring the park, which was like an enormous garden that we shared. She was a very good friend to me.

In the autumn in Hamburg we have a traditional celebration of the end of summer and beginning of winter, called the Lantern Festival. It is, I suppose, a little bit like Hallowe'en, although we didn't go around asking for treats. Children with paper lanterns with candles inside would roam around their neighbourhoods at dusk, singing the lantern song:

> *Laterne, Laterne,*
> *die Sonne, Mond und Sterne,*
> *Meine Laterne die ist so schön,*
> *Da kann man mit ihr spazieren geh'n,*
> *In dem grünen Walde, wo die Büchsen knallen,*
> *Brenne aus mein Licht, brenne aus mein Licht,*
> *Aber nur meine liebe Laterne nicht.*

> (Lantern, lantern,
> the sun, the moon, the stars,
> My lantern is so beautiful,
> That I can go for a walk with it,

Through the green wood where the
    hunters shoot.
Burn to the end, my candle, burn to the
    end, my candle,
But don't set my lantern alight.)

Even in that first autumn after the war, a supply of paper lanterns and candles were somehow found for all of us children. Perhaps the lanterns had been hoarded from before the war, perhaps they were so easy to make that they were quickly available. I don't know where mine came from, but I was delighted to have one, and Karla and I joined all the other park children in our procession around the area, with grown-ups hovering behind us.

The British soldiers were entranced. They had never seen anything like it.

I heard later of prisoners of war finally returning home by train that night. The first sight of Hamburg, their home city, was of ruins, but dotted among them were the lights from all the lantern processions, a tradition they had enjoyed when they themselves were children. It made some of them cry to see how quickly the children of the ravaged

city were getting back to normal, and the little bea-
cons of hope flickering there.

Karla's father, as I said, was very good with his
hands, and he made his daughter a pram and a
beautiful wooden bed for her dolls; and because we
always shared everything, we took it in turns to
have one each: if she had the pram at her house, I
had the bed and vice versa.

That first Christmas in Hammer Park, six months
after we moved there, I was given a proper doll as
my present. She was made of celluloid and had eyes
that closed, and there were coils of plaits moulded
round her head. I immediately christened her
Charlotte, after my beloved lost doll, and I loved
her and played with her endlessly. We were insep-
arable and she helped take my mind off her lost
namesake.

Around Karla's house there were some lovely pear
trees, but they belonged to the park authorities, not
to her family. We would pinch the ones that fell on
the floor, even if they were bruised, but always felt
very naughty and guilty for doing it, although we
relished every mouthful. A large portion of the park
had been given up to make allotments for people

who had no gardens, and we respected their property and never took any of their produce.

There were air raid shelters underneath the park, but the gates to them were locked and we were never tempted to play in them; after my experience in the mine I didn't want to go below ground ever again. More fun was the little bandstand, which had survived the bombing intact, where we used to invent plays and perform them to imaginary audiences. There was a fountain, too, which only worked again when the water shortages were over; in the winter it would freeze into a spectacular ice castle. On the sports fields, which would later be used by my school, we organised impromptu games of rounders, football and handball. There was always a little band of children playing somewhere in the park and compared with those who had to live on the ruined streets it was a blissful place to be.

Just a few years ago, my cousin Henning sent me a book about the history of Hammer Park. He said in his note, 'Read page 126.'

There, among the other contributions to the book, was an article written by Karla about the park

19

A Family Restored

For the first few months after the war, Eva was terribly unhappy.

In August 1945 she worked briefly in a children's hospital in Hamburg, but had to leave after four weeks because the asthma, which plagued her for the rest of her life, became too severe. She had developed asthma after Ruth's death but, remarkably, she was well for the whole duration of our long march. Now it returned with a vengeance and stopped her from working. She became very low and wrote in her diary, 'I don't know why the world does not love me any more.'

In September she went back to Tabarz, to try to claim the possessions she had left behind. It was another adventure, because the trains were still very erratic and she had to travel part of the way on a milk cart. She met some of the other staff and a few of the girls, but the home was closed and, when she got there, all her things had disappeared.

Then came the big disappointment. All my important and precious belongings, which I wanted to take back to Hamburg, had been stolen. I cannot say what a disappointment that was. But what can you do? what is gone is gone.

Her journey back was dangerous, because Tabarz and the whole of that beautiful Thuringia region had been allocated to the Russians when Germany was divided between the Allies. East Germany was now controlled by the Communists and we had heard many tales of the barbaric behaviour of the Russians. She wrote:

ruins and found shards of Mutti's lovely Meissen
dinner service, white with a gold rim. But the
looters had long since taken anything worth sal-
vaging and who can blame them? They had to make
homes among the debris, so they naturally took
anything they could find that was serviceable. If
Mutti was upset by what she saw she didn't show
it. And I know from talking to her in later years,
when I was an adult, that she really did not feel the
loss of a home acutely, because she had learned
what real loss was with the death of Ruth.

Eva next had a job with a dentist, as a recep-
tionist, but this only lasted four weeks because she
was ill again. To help with her asthma she joined
a walking group of twenty to thirty people who
went on regular excursions to the Lüneburg Heath.
I was sometimes allowed to go with her, if the walk
was not going to be too strenuous. She obviously
didn't mind that we were walking in the same area
where we had our devastating encounter with the
plunderers, or she wouldn't have chosen to go.
Neither of us had been put off walking by our long
expedition. In fact, I used to love those days out,
because they reminded me of the nice parts of our

adventure, and when we stopped for lunch or tea I got to taste the wonderful heath honey again.

———————

As the long months after the war wore on it seemed less and less likely that my father would ever return. When 1945 became 1946, the trains delivering ex-servicemen and ex-prisoners from the Russian camps slowed to a trickle. Mutti and Eva deliberately talked less and less to me about Father, because they wanted to prepare me for the fact that he might never return. But when they were alone together they kept their memories of him alive and lived day to day in hope that there might still be good news.

On 15 September 1946, a full sixteen months after the end of the war, a letter came. To our astonishment it was from Father — he was alive. There was great celebration in the house. Even Mutti had almost given up hope, as most of the prisoners of war had now returned and all around us there were families happy to be reunited, or mourning the loss of a father or son. Father's brief message told us that he was in a camp in Mühlhausen in Thuringia, having been sent there from the prisoner-of-war camp in Murmansk, in the very north of the USSR, for medical examination and quarantine before being allowed home. By coincidence, Mühlhausen is only a few miles from Tabarz.

When she heard the news, Mutti cried and laughed, and Eva and I joined in, dancing round our little living room. Father's fiftieth birthday was on 28 September and we prayed that he would be back by then. I was secretly praying that he would be back for my ninth birthday on the 20 September.

Eva wrote in her diary:

How will he be when he gets back? I don't really care, as long as he makes it home, even if we have to look after him for a long time. The main thing is that he will be back with us. As long as Mr W. provides us with fruit, vegetables and potatoes, we can make sure we get him back to good health.

It was a real worry: we had seen others return from the Russian prisoner-of-war camps emaciated, with a yellow tinge to their skin, hollow cheeks and strange tufts of hair beginning to reappear on their shaved heads. Getting them back to normal required gradual and careful feeding, and tender loving care. We were all prepared to do anything it took to get Father well, but we were dreading seeing him in that condition.

One afternoon, on 25 September, I was playing in the bedroom I shared with Eva at the back of our house when a strange man peered in through the window at me. I ran out of the room, shouting, 'Mutti, Mutti, there is a man coming here! There is a man in our garden!'

I really did not recognise my father. I was so young and had not seen him for two years, and he was thin and changed. But Mutti knew who it must be. She gasped and ran out of the door to fling herself into his arms, and they held each other for ages before he hugged me. 'Hello, Bärbel,' he said, smiling and kissing me. 'Do you remember your old father?'

Now I did, and I cried too, so happy to see my father home with us. He sat with Mutti and me in the sitting room, telling us what had happened to him. Then we heard Eva's footsteps coming up the path. Father stood up and as she came into the room she saw him and gasped with astonishment. Without a word, he took Eva into his arms and hugged her and hugged her. None of us could speak, we all had tears streaming down our faces, just as I have now when I remember it.

I couldn't imagine anything better than all of us being back together again.

Father was very, very thin, but not in as bad shape as some other survivors. He never talked very much about what he had seen and endured in the camp, but we know he witnessed the death of many friends. He told us that when he was first taken to the camp he lied and told the Russians he had been in the catering corps. This probably saved his life, because they put him to work in the kitchens. After his hand was injured in the First World War, a physiotherapist told him to exercise it by kneading bread, so he was used to that. (I remember that he used to make delicious plum bread in the Wandsbecker Chaussee.) The rest of the cooking involved boiling vegetables, which was not difficult, so his lack of catering skills was never noticed. The kitchens were the warmest place in the camp and the kitchen staff had access to supplies, which they could use to help other prisoners. So although he was half starved, he was better off than most. He gave me a silver knife, a gift from another prisoner who was grateful for some extra food Father had managed to smuggle to him. I still have it and I use it every day. Murmansk, where he was imprisoned, is so far north that it is inside the Arctic Circle. He told me it was dark for almost the whole day and colder than he could have ever imagined.

We told Father all about our long walk, and he was astonished and very proud of our achievement. We often talked of the adventures we had had along the way, especially the funny bits. We did not speak of the dark and dangerous parts of our story, focusing only on the kindness and generosity of the many people we had met.

Father's recovery was slow but steady. I can remember him once going out for a walk, leaning on Mutti for support. We went to the restaurant in the centre of Hammer Park, which was run by a family Mutti had got to know quite well. (The father, before his marriage, had been the valet of

Pope Pius XII.) My parents sat there and drank shandy together. Then Father went to the counter and said, 'Twenty cigarettes, please.'

The girl behind the counter looked at him in astonishment.

'Waldi,' said my mother gently, 'cigarettes are on ration. They are vastly expensive. I doubt you will be able to afford twenty of them!'

In fact, he could only afford two. They were also terrible, not at all like the ones they were used to smoking before the war. Father had no idea.

Before long, he started growing tobacco plants in our garden and I can still see the leaves strung up and hanging in our shed to dry out, before they were made into 'tobacco' and rolled into cigarettes.

At that time cigarettes were an unofficial currency. The British soldiers got bigger rations of them than the Germans and they would exchange them: twenty cigarettes for a watch, fifty for a camera and so on. Soap was also very scarce, and again the troops had more and could barter with it.

All food was on ration and things were very difficult for those first two winters after the war. Fuel ran out, although we were lucky and could collect branches fallen from the park trees. When the park wardens cut down a tree they would not bother with the roots, so Father and some of the other men would dig them out, which was back-breaking work. But it was worth it once they dried them out and could use them for fuel. In some areas of the city all the trees were cut down for burning. I was blissfully unaware of all these privations, because as a child I was always given a full plate of food. Other people in my family probably went hungry to make sure I was well fed, because I was the only one who was still growing. And because my mother was such a good cook, she was very inventive and found lots of ways of making our meagre rations appetising.

While we were establishing ourselves in the little house in Hammer Park, the rest of our family were also finding their feet back in Hamburg. Because they were old, Opa and Omi, my grandparents, were found an apartment quickly. It was close to a railway station, so when we visited them I loved being allowed to run on ahead and press the bell. I remember there was a huge mahogany chest of drawers in the bedroom (donated, probably, by one

they were reunited with Uncle Willi, they built their own house on the plot of land that was their share of my grandfather's lottery win. So it had been a very wise choice after all, now that my mother's china was smashed and Aunt Irma's jewellery had long since been stolen in all the looting. They worked hard on it and built their house themselves. It must be very satisfying for my cousin Thekla, who still lives there, to know that she helped build her own home.

Uncle Willi was a very practical man, who could tackle anything, a real jack of all trades. He was an amateur boxer and the family lived very close to the famous German world champion heavyweight, Max Schmeling, who was a friend. Uncle Willi and Max Schmeling even sparred together. (Max Schmeling outlived Uncle Willi by many years, dying in 2005 at the age of ninety-nine.) We would sometimes be allowed to go to the gym to see Uncle Willi in the ring and those were always very exciting days. Sadly, Uncle Willi died early, in 1959, when he was only fifty-seven years old.

Despite everything they had suffered during the war, the adults focused on getting back to a normal life, for themselves but, most of all, for us, the children. Before the war the family had always held literary evenings once a month, which they took it in turn to host. Everyone was expected to read something: a poem or an excerpt from a book, and then talk about it. Sometimes it would be a song, especially for us little ones. It was a lovely tradition and it kept the family very close, and as soon as we all had our own homes it started again.

There were other evenings when the adults played cards. We children, Volker, Henning and I, used to hope that Uncle Hermann would win, because he always gave his winnings to us and it was, in our terms, quite a lot of money. He was a seafaring engineer and after the war he worked on whaling ships. We had some stunning photographs of him and his crewmates, with icicles hanging from their eyebrows and moustaches. He allowed me to take the photographs to school and do a presentation for my classmates about his life at sea.

But usually the card games were won by Father, who had a very sharp mind and could easily work out which cards had already been played. When he was sufficiently recovered, he started work again for the railways, but now he had a desk job in Hamburg, without any travelling. He stayed there until he got his pension.

Four months after Father's return, things began to look up for Eva. She and two friends used to visit a temporary military hospital in a collection of Nissen huts in Harburg, to read to soldiers who were recovering from war injuries, or to write letters for those too disabled to do it themselves. It was there, on 17 January 1947, as her diary records, that she met Kurt, who came originally from the German part of Romania, Siebenbürgen. He had not been injured, but he was so malnourished that he needed care and convalescence.

Kurt and Eva fell deeply in love and stayed that way until Eva's death in 1990. Everything she had written in her diary, all that poignant longing for a man to love and be with and look after, came true for Eva. She and Kurt were so happy together. When he was transferred for more convalescence to a home at St Andreasberg, in the beautiful Hartz mountains, she travelled there to see him.

It did not take them long to realise their feelings for each other and she wrote:

I love Kurt so much, I cannot imagine being away from him.

She made her last diary entry in April 1947. It read:

Happiness and sunshine have finally come my way.

They were married almost a year after they met, on 29 November 1947. It was hugely exciting for me, because I was the bridesmaid. I had what I would now think was a strange dress, but at the time I thought it was the most beautiful creation ever made. We were sent care parcels from Britain and the USA, and in them we sometimes received material. My mother was a brilliant needlewoman and she made me an off-white satin top, with long sleeves, beautifully smocked. There was not enough fabric for the skirt, so she made that in light-blue patterned satin. I was so thrilled with it that I preened and twirled like a catwalk model.

Eva had a traditional white wedding dress that the daughter of one of mother's cousins had worn, and with a few small alterations it fitted her perfectly.

It was a beautiful November day when they married, cold but bright and sunny. The whole family came to celebrate Eva's wedding. They had their legal marriage ceremony in a register office, then went to church for a blessing. Afterwards, we walked through Hammer Park in a little procession to the restaurant, where we had a lovely meal. We toasted the happy couple with Sekt, which is German champagne, and even I was allowed a small glass. It was a day of great laughter and happiness, because we all loved Kurt almost as much as Eva did and were so happy he was to be a part of our family.

Eva's and Kurt's first home was in the cellar of a bombed-out house in a road opposite Hammer Park. The entrance door to the cellar was still there and there were steps down into it. The walls and ceiling were sound, although our father was always afraid the ruins would collapse on top of them, and when it rained they had to put buckets and bowls around the place to catch the drips. There were no windows, but they made it into a beautiful home and I used to love going there. I had my own little room, which I was very proud of. One night I woke up and, half awake and half asleep, went looking for the toilet. Eva found me trying to climb on top of a chest of drawers. I remember her taking hold of me, shaking me gently and saying, 'Wake up, Puppe, darling,' which is what she always used to say when she needed to get me up after the air raid warnings during our walk.

When Eva became pregnant, she and Kurt decided the cellar was not a good place to bring up a baby. They rented an apartment in Flottbek, part of a large villa with beautiful gardens. Kurt worked for a very upmarket shop in Othmarschen, a posh area of Hamburg. It sold crockery, pots, pans and all sorts of other things. Kurt could do everything: he was an electrician, a plumber and a handyman.

Later they bought a big house in the same area, with help from Kurt's employers, a lovely couple who had lost their own sons in the war and who treated Kurt like a surrogate son. It was big enough for them to let out rooms to students in later years.

Kurt and Eva were so right together. As a child I always felt that if I could find a husband as good as Kurt I would be happy. He could play the accordion by ear, which impressed me greatly at that age. When their first daughter, Angelika, was born in 1948 Eva was only seven months pregnant and the baby weighed two pounds. She was so small that I had her baby clothes afterwards for my dolls. Gunda, their second daughter, was born three years later.

Although my mother could make clothes out of any scraps of material, and adapt and alter things to fit us, shoes were a real problem. There were none to be had, for love nor money. Eva's Kurt came to our rescue. He would buy large sheets of compressed rubber, which he cut to the size of our feet, using our old shoes as a template. He even added a small heel at the back. Then he punched holes round the edges and threaded through strips of leather, cut from old coats. These went across our feet, and one strip went round our ankles and fastened with a buckle. I have a photograph of myself, taken in 1948, sitting on the wall outside my high school wearing them – I always sat on the wall outside waiting for my best friends to arrive before lessons. Not many years ago, on holiday in the Canary Islands, I fell into conversation with an elderly German couple who had lived opposite the high school in Hamburg. They knew Aunt Käte, who lived nearby. They remembered the girl with fair curly hair who sat on the wall with her distinctive sandals. It is, as I have often had occasion to observe, a small world.

The sandals were very comfortable and looked good: there was always a lot of demand from friends and family for Kurt to make them, and his fingers were often numb and blistered from stitching the difficult material.

Mutti's skills as a seamstress meant she spent one day a month at the home of one of her cousins, the one who owned the plant nurseries, repairing, lengthening, shortening and adapting clothes for their three young boys. She would unpick the frayed collars of shirts and turn them over, to give the garment a new life. The family were reasonably wealthy, but no amount of money could buy clothes, which simply were not in the shops. They did not pay Mutti, but she and I would get lovely food while we were there because they had land to grow things and there were farms around — as ever, those who lived in the countryside fared better than those in the city. We took the precious parcels back home with us.

Times were hard but we looked forwards, not backwards. Mutti kept up the pragmatism and stoicism that Eva displayed during our long march, and always talked about the new Hamburg that would rise from the ashes and how lucky we were that a modern city was going to take shape. Her attitude, which she imbued into me, was that all we had lost were possessions and they were unimportant. Our family was intact and our spirits were strong.

Growing Up

20

Growing Up

Eventually, after our endless holiday, school did restart for all of us. A kindergarten was established in a temporary building, donated by Denmark, in the park itself, but of course I was too old for that. The elementary school was quite a long way from the park, but in those days children were trusted to walk on their own. Karla, another friend Helga, who lived in the same row of houses as me, and I made our way together, walking through devastated streets. In some places we saw faded messages scrawled on walls, telling a husband or a son or a daughter that the family had survived and where they had moved to. I wonder how many of those messages were written in vain and how many of those husbands or children made it back to be reunited with their families? There were signs on the rubble saying that looters would be prosecuted, but by this time there was nothing left worth looting. Even the timbers used in the construction of the buildings had all been taken for firewood or floorboards.

We explored some of the smaller houses and I dare say that if we had found anything worth having we would have kept it — but there was nothing left at all. We were told by our mothers not to go into the ruins, as they could obviously be dangerous, but the temptation was sometimes too strong. It was an adventure. We didn't think of the tumbled-down structures, where rats and feral cats lived, as the wreckage of people's lives but as a fascinating playground.

School started early at 8 a.m. We all took along our own metal basins and spoons, and we were given a meal mid morning. Two children from every class were picked to have extra food, as they were particularly undernourished. I was one at first, but I hated being different from my classmates and gladly relinquished the 'honour'. School finished at around 1 p.m. so we were home for lunch, which meant we were all getting an extra meal a day to help build us up. In the afternoon we could go to extra lessons – music, dancing and gymnastics – but we had to pay for these.

When I was nine I contracted polio, probably from swimming in the River Elbe. We'd been to visit relatives who lived near the river bank and I went for a swim. Within twenty-four hours I was terribly sick, vomiting and hardly able to move my body. I was admitted to the local hospital, then transferred to the big children's hospital, where I was diagnosed with polio. I spent two months in hospital, but, to my great good fortune, I was one of the first victims of the disease in Germany to be treated with a new American serum. My parents had to give permission for it to be tried on me and I'm so glad they did because I recovered without any ill effects. It took several months for me to get back to normal and I had to struggle to regain my fitness, but I forced myself to go to gym club and ballet lessons, until I was back to my earlier form. It is another reason I have to thank the Americans.

My classmates were grateful to me: because the disease is infectious they were all given a fortnight off school, until it was clear that none of them had caught it from me.

Four years later I was dangerously ill again, this time with meningitis. I really thought I would die. I had a blinding headache, I was vomiting, I couldn't hold up my head and bright spots swam before my eyes. I was rushed into hospital again, and my fear that I was dying was confirmed when my parents came to visit me and brought me a watch. I had always asked for a watch or a bicycle for my birthday and Christmas presents, but they told me that because I was such a tomboy I would hurt myself on a bike and break a watch. So when they turned up with a watch, I was sure it meant that the end was near for me and they were granting me my last wish. I started to cry, but I couldn't tell them why.

I was really ill and crying was the worst thing, as it agitated the inflamed tissues of my brain even more. But then a good-looking young doctor came and sat on my bed and took my hand. He said, 'I'm new here, I've only just started working as a doctor and I have to prove myself. I really want to get you better but I can't do it on my own. I need you to help me. We can do it together.'

He calmed me down and I fell asleep, my first proper, deep sleep since I became ill. When I woke up, he was sitting on my bed again – at first I thought he must have been there the whole time. That was the turning point and I started to get better. I had to have several lumbar punctures, in which a long needle, almost a foot long I seem to remember, was inserted to remove fluid from around my spinal cord. I used to think, 'If they're not careful, this needle will come out of my belly button in the front.' Afterwards I had to lie flat on my back without pillows for twenty-four hours, to prevent me developing headaches. Again, I was in hospital for several weeks.

One day, when I was getting better, the nurses dressed me up in one of their uniforms. When my parents came in to see me, my bed was empty but as they walked through the door I came up behind them and said, 'Can I help you?' They were really surprised that I was well enough to play tricks on them.

My classmates were thrilled to get two more weeks off school because, again, meningitis is infectious. When I got back to school they asked me, 'What is your next illness? Come on, we all want another two weeks' holiday.'

I told them it must be someone else's turn. 'I've done my share – I want two weeks off now.'

But it never happened.

When I was ten I passed an exam, which meant I could go to the high school that was the equivalent of a grammar school here. The little house in the park was very close to my new high school – I could practically hear the morning bell from my home – and it was great not having to walk far. The boys' high school was still being used as a hospital, so they were given the upper floors of our building, but strenuous efforts were made to ensure that the girls and boys never met and mingled. It was only at dancing classes, held after school, that we got to know any boys.

My after-school hours were fully booked with a programme of activities. As well as gym and ballroom-dancing classes, I also went to 'movement with music' classes, which were like ballet except that we didn't stand on pointes. The teacher was a very effeminate chap whose name, Bodo, made us giggle. But I was always very proud to be chosen to demonstrate with him.

I made three really great friends at high school, Ilse, Antje and Karin. Ilse's mother was a war widow struggling to bring up three children by running a confectionery shop, which we passed on the way to school. We four made ourselves into a special little club and we called ourselves CDS. We never told anyone what it stood for and, even though Antje and Karin are both now dead, I will still not reveal it. (Ilse and I are in close contact and I see her whenever I visit Hamburg.) Both Antje and Karin came from fairly wealthy families, living in villas outside the city, but I never felt disadvantaged because we had lost everything in the war. Once when Antje, who was very good at sport, damaged her leg badly falling over the finishing line in a 100-metre sprint, she stayed with us because we were so close to the school. She left behind her beautiful villa for our little cottage without a bathroom, but she was very happy with us. Mutti was a real homemaker, who made everyone welcome.

An English student teacher, Daphne Asplin, came to Hamburg to give us English lessons. The school appealed for families to put her up for a month at a time. Although our house was small and there were other girls in the school with substantially better accommodation to offer her, she liked it so much with us that she stayed for not just one month but two. (I am still in touch with her. She never became a teacher because she realised she would always have favourites among her pupils, so she worked for the Foreign Office in London instead.)

I was always top at English in school and for that I thank the British soldiers who educated me so well in the language. I was very keen to go to England and we had a school exchange with Leigh Grammar School in Atherton, Lancashire. I remember it rained a fine drizzle for most of the two weeks we were there in August 1954. We had little tennis dresses and we wanted to show off in them, but the weather was rarely good enough. I thought the men looked very strange, because they wore suits with back vents in the jackets, which made their bottoms seem to stick out.

When I got home I said to my mother, 'Whatever happens in my life, I will never, ever marry an Englishman.' She often teased me about that, after I married not one, but two, Englishmen.

Luckily, the trip was a success, despite the bad weather; we got on well with the English girls and it did not put me off wanting to go back. I even had my name in the local paper there, because a reporter came to a party that was given for us and asked for our impressions of England. Four girls and four boys, out of the thirty on the trip, were quoted in the paper. We girls focused on trivial but telling differences between the two countries: open fires, thick carpets and orderly queues for buses impressed us most. The boys talked rather more seriously about the relationship between the two nations.

I stayed with a lovely family: a girl called Marion Archer, who was the same age as me, her parents and younger sister. I was introduced to cricket for the first time and was completely baffled by it to begin with. (In later life I came really to appreciate the game and am a great supporter of the England team.)

I inherited all my mother's and grandmother's skill at knitting, crocheting and sewing, and my nickname at school was *Strickpuppe*, knitted doll, because I knitted so many of my own clothes. Unlike English schoolgirls, we didn't have to wear a uniform. I knitted one skirt that was so full that when I spun round, it flared out to waist level. It was green, with rows of little brown rabbit heads round the hem, and I embroidered ears on every rabbit. Later, when I was old enough to go out socially, one of my friends, Ursi, would come round and we would make ourselves new dresses in one evening.

When I was eighteen, after the German equivalent of A-levels, I came over to England to study the language. Father was always very protective of me, perhaps because we had spent so long apart in the war. He always called me '*kleine Bärbel*' (little Bärbel) and as a teenager I used to chafe at his early curfews. One night he stayed up all night, falling asleep in an armchair, because he thought I was still out. In the morning he went to Mutti, very worried that

I had not come home, to be told by her that I had changed my mind about going out and had gone to bed for an early night. Despite this, he was happy to let me go off for my studies, because Ilse was coming with me.

I attended a language centre in Oxford Street, London, to learn English and French, and after that passed the 'lower' and 'proficiency' certificates in English from the University of Cambridge. My accommodation was arranged by Daphne Asplin and I stayed with a wonderful couple, Mr and Mrs Lawson, in St John's Wood. They are now quite elderly and I am still in touch with them.

Most people in England were very welcoming, but there was some suspicion of Ilse and me because we were German. We were sitting on the long seat at the back of a double-decker bus once, talking together in German, and a man threw tomatoes at us. I could understand that people still felt hurt and angry about the war, but I spoke up and said in English, which by now was quite good, that I had been two when the war started and seven when it ended, so it could not be anything to do with me.

We were sometimes accused of being Nazis and

when we protested that we weren't we were told that all Germans were Nazis. I usually dealt with it by making clear how sorry we were for what had happened.

After a year in London I went to university in Geneva, accompanied this time by another friend, Ursula. I graduated in English, French and Literature. The international student accommodation was at the top of a hill, in an old building with cloisters and arches everywhere. It was run as a benevolent dictatorship by Madame Müller. We got on well with her, always making sure we cleared up after our breakfasts and giving her little presents. Nonetheless, when we were summoned to see her after our first term we were really worried. Was our room too much of a mess? Had we come in late and been reported to her?

But we were not in trouble. She explained to us that she had a new student who had arrived from Israel with her father. Her name was Miriam and the family were Jewish. Her parents, both dentists, had fled Germany at the beginning of the war and, although Miriam had been born there, she had grown up in Israel. She knew what the Germans had done to the Jews and, as a consequence, she refused to speak German or read German literature. Her parents were upset by this: after all, German was their mother tongue and they would have liked their daughter to speak it. They also knew that only a very small percentage of Germans were implicated in the Holocaust, that most people were honest and decent, and that the language was that of some of the world's most beautiful literature and poetry.

'Her father wants her to learn that there are good Germans. So will you agree to having another bed in your room?' Madame Müller asked.

We agreed and Miriam became a great friend. She, Ursula and I formed a very tight bond and we became like sisters. We taught her German, giving her dictation every day, so that she could speak to her parents in their own language. They were so grateful that we became such good friends. We did not really know the full story of the Holocaust ourselves: I think the truth was too painful for our nation to admit and, although it was touched on, it was never openly discussed. Miriam is now a Professor of Languages and Islamic Law at the

Hebrew University of Jerusalem. She has written many erudite books and always sends me one, writing in the front '*Meine kleine Schwester Bärbel*', my little sister Bärbel.

Ursula went on to marry a Jewish man and much later, when he died he left his coin collection to a museum in Jerusalem, so just after his funeral we went out there and stayed with Miriam for the opening of the collection to the public.

After I graduated I was going to become a teacher. Mutti was very keen on this as she said that when I had my own children I would be able to have the same holidays as they did. But on my flight back to Hamburg from Geneva I found my new career. I chatted on the plane to the Lufthansa stewardesses and I was attracted to the life they led, visiting so many places. They told me how to apply to work for the airline. My career was about to take off.

21

England

Before I went to Geneva we were living in a new apartment in old Horn, an area of Hamburg close to Hammer Park. It was a spacious, two-bedroom flat in a beautiful new landscaped complex, part of the rebuilding of Hamburg into the stunning modern city that my mother had predicted would emerge from the ruins in time. My bedroom had a balcony overlooking the well-tended gardens. It was our second home since the prefab in Hammer Park, which we left in 1954 (a year before they were all pulled down). First we moved to Tyrolerstrasse, an area that Mutti didn't like, so fortunately we didn't stay there long. We soon moved back to the part of the city she did like, which was close to her sisters, and to our beloved Hammer Park.

It was at this time that I lost my dear grandparents. Both of them had remained mentally sharp until the end of their lives and we were all very close, visiting often. My grandfather died three or four years before my grandmother. I was sixteen when Omi died. She was seventy-four and her death left a great void in my life. I miss her still. They are buried in the family grave at Ohlsdorf, in the plot bought first for Ruth. Now it is the resting place of many others — my mother and father, Eva, Aunt Irma, Uncle Hermann, Aunt Hilda and Uncle Willi are all buried there. My cousins Thekla and Henning care for and maintain the grave.

When I arrived home from university in Geneva I was feeling restless, so on impulse I dressed in my best outfit and went to the Lufthansa offices at the airport to see if I could get an interview. I didn't have an appointment but I was lucky and they saw me. I had to do a battery of psychological tests, which I obviously passed with flying colours, because they rang me the next day to arrange for another interview. The fact that I could speak German, English and French fluently was a big mark in my favour. I was offered a job in the department dealing with customers' complaints, based in Hamburg.

At this time I was seeing Ingo, my first and only German boyfriend. He was two years younger than me, so I always feared he might meet a girl of his own age, because when you are that young, two years is a big gap. We had remained close all the time I was away in Geneva. We were deeply in love, but we never made love: in those days girls saved themselves for marriage and Ingo was too much of a gentleman ever to try to compromise me. I was remarkably innocent. Once, when I was at a sports day, I was watching a long-distance race and the boy who came first had an erection, which showed in his running shorts. I had no idea what it was and was sure there was something seriously wrong with him. I worried about it for a few days, then mentioned it to Eva. She laughed and explained it all to me, that it was caused by excitement and would soon go away. When she told me the purpose of erections I was shocked: until then I had thought you got pregnant from French kissing.

I would have gone to the ends of the earth for Ingo, who was training to be an engineer. He was very good-looking and reminded me of the soldier who rescued me when I rolled down the hill. He had a wonderful way of explaining things, whether they were technical, mechanical or philosophical. I still have all his letters and all the presents he ever gave me. I treasure a red leather folder for keeping letters in and a brown leather vanity case, as well as the books he gave me. We went on holidays together with my sister and her family, and his mother, a widow, and his sister Heide. Like me, he was very family orientated.

After much heart-searching, Ingo and I decided we should try being apart for a while to make up our minds about each other. We ended up being separated for two years and, sadly for me, he did meet someone else. I was heartbroken, but felt that we had obviously done the right thing. That's when I decided that I wanted to leave Hamburg and make a completely fresh start.

In my job it wasn't difficult to arrange. I was transferred to Frankfurt and then offered a job in San Francisco. I needed to arrange a US visa and my cousin Ulrich, who was by then living in the States, sponsored me. In the meantime I was sent on a temporary posting to London and while there I was offered a permanent place in England with Lufthansa. I had to choose between America and England, which was not easy, as I was really drawn to both countries. My mother always joked that the stork put me in the wrong nest and that I should have been born in England or America. I chose London, simply because it was so much nearer for visiting my family, and my father was not well.

Before I left Germany, my mother gave me a leather-bound notebook. I took my lead from Eva and began to write down poems, quotations, extracts from books I was reading, as well as keeping pressed flowers and even a four-leafed clover in there. The very first thing I wrote was from a seventeenth-century writer, John Amos Comenius, and I chose it because I was still so close to the war and its aftermath:

Why should we look down on other races? We are all human beings, of one world and of one blood. To hate a person just because he was born somewhere else, just because he speaks a different language, just because he thinks about things in a different way, does not make sense. We should get away from that. We are all people, nobody is perfect, and we all need help.

I believed then, and I believe now, that if everyone kept this in their heart, the world would be a better place. My own heart was still full of my love for Ingo and I wrote a sad poem about our separation. It flows a little better in German but I include the English translation here, as it captures so much of how I felt at the time:

> My love for you is always yours,
> It will engulf all your uncertainties,
> It will protect you always, lovingly and
>   magnificently,
> Its strength and might are without
>   boundaries,

From all your troubles and worries you
   can flee into its solitude.
My thoughts are all around you,
Your heart will find its rest,
Lovingly, I melt myself into you.

In London, I became resigned to losing Ingo and
was determined to make the best of my new life. I
wrote, 'Before you go to bed, give your troubles to
God. He will be up all night anyway.'

I did a variety of jobs for Lufthansa in London,
sharing a flat in Eaton Square with two girlfriends,
close enough for me to be able to walk to the airline offices in Old Bond Street. Before long I met
Michael, who worked for Scandinavian Airline
Systems (SAS). He was the epitome of an Englishman: he wore a camel coat, played cricket at weekends and socialised at his cricket club. We quickly
fell in love, and within seven months we were
engaged and married four months after that. We were
married in a register office and went to Hamburg to
have the wedding blessed at the Hammer Church,
the Dreifaltigkeitskirche. The original building,
where I was christened, had been destroyed in the

bombing and for a few years we used a wooden temporary church, which was where I was confirmed and where Eva was married in 1947. I sang in the choir there for many years. By the time I married, on 16 March 1963 at the age of twenty-five, a splendid new church had been built.

I loved setting up my own first home. I would have done it anywhere, but England already felt like home to me and it was near enough to Germany for me to see my family, so I didn't regret living in another country. I kept in close touch with them, especially Mutti and Eva – we often wrote, talked and visited each other.

A year after my wedding I had my first child, Michael, who was born on 21 March 1964. Even after I got married, I was still remarkably naive compared with girls today. Just before my wedding, my mother gave me a little gadget that looked like an egg timer. I asked her what it was for and she said that I should put into it the dates of my periods, and it would tell me when it was safe to make love. It failed to work.

I didn't mind getting pregnant so soon, as I had always believed that I wanted to have children, build a home and live happily ever after – all the things that Eva yearned for so wistfully in her wartime diary.

While I was pregnant with Michael, I went to an antenatal clinic and the doctor asked me if I had ever had German measles.

'Well, I have had measles and I was in Germany – does that make them German measles?' I asked, which made him laugh.

Michael was a beautiful baby. I know all mothers say that, but it really was true in his case. I gave up work to look after him, and every summer my mother and father would come across, and my father would stay with me for three months until Mutti came back again to take him home. He had had seven strokes and was partially paralysed, so I looked after him to give her a break. Although he spoke no English, he enjoyed his trips. My husband got on well with him despite the language barrier: they both enjoyed a flutter on racehorses, which gave them a lingua franca.

My baby Meiki (I always called Michael 'Meiki') helped me 'sting' my father for a large amount of money. I was changing a nappy and, emulating what Eva did with her babies, even though he was only three months old I held him over the potty before I put the clean nappy on. Father laughed and said I'd be very lucky if he did anything – and added that he would give me £10 if Meiki managed to do both things. To my great surprise, Meiki promptly did. I told him for years afterwards that he started earning money at three months old, and good money because £10 then was worth more than £100 today. The following day I asked my father if he wanted to bet again, but he said no, emphatically.

My daughter Babette was born on 1 July 1966. I really concentrated on keeping her in the womb because I was determined she would not be born in June, as that would have meant the last three digits of her date of birth were 666 and someone had told me they were the devil's numbers. She was born in the early hours of the morning, so I only just made it. She weighed a whole pound less than Meiki and looked scrawny, like a little skinned rabbit. When he first saw her my husband said, 'That can't be my baby,' but I had to tell him she was. Aunt Hilda said the nicest thing: she said Babette looked like 'an Oriental princess'. She has certainly grown up to be

kept kicking their football into the middle of a new flower bed I was trying to establish, with tender young plants. I opened the bedroom window and shouted to Meiki to be more careful where they kicked the ball. I spoke to him in German – he grew up fluent in it. Babette understands it but doesn't really speak it very much. Meiki's friend looked at me in astonishment, not understanding anything I was saying. Meiki said to him, 'It's all right, my mother is German. But she's quite nice really.'

Another time he was playing with his toy soldiers and I walked into the room just as he was muttering to himself about shooting all the Germans. He caught sight of me and hastily changed it to 'Japanese'.

When the children were both at school, I applied to the German Food Centre in Knightsbridge and was taken on as a home economist. It was a great job because I could work my hours around the children. My boss knew that if he gave me something to do, it would get done well. I had a very good friend, Edith, the wife of one of my husband's colleagues who was godmother to both Meiki and Babette. She was always happy to step in to look after them if I had to be away overnight. Edith only lived 600 yards from us, so it worked out very well. She is still a good friend and stays with us weekly.

At this time I also met one of my dearest friends, Maria, who is Austrian, and is like a sister to me. She, too, was married to an Englishman and we clicked as soon as we met. We have been great friends for thirty-five years and now she lives two roads away from us. I am very good at keeping and nurturing my friendships, and I sometimes wonder whether it is because, when Eva and I were on our long march, we met people who became close for a short time and then we never saw or heard from them again. That was what war was like and perhaps that is why I value my solid, long-standing relationships now.

I worked for the German Food Centre until it closed down in 1988 and it was a fascinating time. My job was to organise big promotions, cooking demonstrations, stands at fairs, give lectures on German food and drink, set up delicatessens in big stores and so on. I and the other girls always dressed in German national dress. I met lots of celebrities. I met Prince Charles at the Royal Show at Kenilworth

later became my second husband. Ray was also married when we met, with four young sons, Stephen, David, Andrew and Matthew, so it was a traumatic time for all of us, but everything worked out well.

He was born in the Forest of Dean seventeen months after I was born in Hamburg (I refer to him as my toyboy). He was one of nine children and his mother, a widow, brought them all up in a two-bedroomed cottage. The whole family was musical, all his brothers and sisters sing, and some of them play musical instruments. His two older brothers used to sing at local concerts and at big family parties, and they took Ray along as a mascot. The first time he sang in public he was only five or six years old, and he insisted on turning his back to the audience because he didn't want to look at them.

He learned to play the cornet and the trumpet in a local brass band. After he left school he worked in a sawmill, which he hated, and later trained as a manager at the Co-op. Like all young men in those days, he was called up to do two years' national service. He was originally in the army catering corps, but when he became a regular soldier and they realised he had musical ability, he transferred to the Royal Army Service Corps, which later became the Royal Corps of Transport Band. After that, he joined the band of the Welsh Guards. Although he played the trumpet and cornet, his main instrument was his voice, so he was the official vocalist for the band – we have many records on which the bands are featured.

Ray was in the army when we met. As well as my career with the German Food Centre, I also did private catering and I got to know the bands who provided entertainment at these functions as I was sometimes asked to co-ordinate the music as well as the food. Ray played in his spare time with a group of his fellow army bandsmen in a band called the New Clubmen (an earlier band had been the Clubmen). He was the vocalist and compère.

I was putting on a function for the German Food Centre and we needed a German oompah band to play at it, so I asked Ray if he and his friends would do it, which they did, very well. From then on we worked together many times, doing promotions for BMW cars and motorbikes, Mercedes Benz, Holsten lager, Löwenbräu beer and so on.

I told him he should set up his own band, which

he did, calling it the Rupert Hentzau Bier Band, the name taken from the main character in *The Prisoner of Zenda*. They didn't only play German music: there was always a medley of English favourites like 'Roll Out the Barrel' and 'Down at the Old Bull and Bush', so that everyone could join in the singing if they wanted to.

Gradually our feelings for each other developed and eventually we knew we had to be together. There were painful times as our two families changed and reassembled, but after five years together we married in 1984. Ray was not happy living in my old family home, so we bought a beautiful cottage at Hinchley Wood. My ex-husband and Ray got on well, and when he came to pick up the children they would play table tennis tournaments with them in the garden.

My son Michael, and one of Ray's sons, David, both had music lessons in drumming from a friend of Ray's from the Welsh Guards band.

Ray and I worked very hard: at the start, he had his army commitments, and spent his evenings and weekends with his band. I used to do the private catering at the same events, as well as my job.

Sundays were our only free time, when we could be together and relax. I once said to Ray, 'I love Sundays.'

He replied, very romantically, 'With you, every day is Sunday.'

Then, even more romantically, he went to the piano and composed a piece of music for me, called 'Every Day is Sunday', which he gave me on our anniversary instead of a card. He plays it to me often. He loves sitting at the piano, playing and singing, and I love listening to him.

He left the army in 1981, a few months after playing for Prince Charles as he came out of Buckingham Palace on his way to St Paul's Cathedral to marry Princess Diana. He has always said how relieved he was to be playing at the beginning of that day, because afterwards he and the others could take off their dress uniforms and relax, whereas other bands had to wait until the end of the ceremony to perform.

After twenty-three and a half years' service, Ray left the army and became the building super-intendent for an office block in Piccadilly, which gave us the use of a flat right in the heart of London.

We had our family commitments, but we were still able to spend time there. By now the children were teenagers and loved to be able to stay in central London. It was a happy, busy life.

colleague called Joanie out in New England. Before long they were exchanging photographs and eventually, about twelve months later, Joanie took the initiative and asked Meiki what he was doing for his summer holidays, as she had to go to her best friend Debs's wedding in Cape Cod and she needed an escort.

He flew out to the States for two weeks and some time later she flew over here and met us, and it was clear they were really smitten with each other. Before long, they were flying backwards and forwards every month, so they decided they needed to be together. Joanie and Meiki took a year out to travel all over the world, meeting their extended families, before they eventually decided to settle back in the States.

It was a wrench when Meiki left England to live so far away, but I saw how happy he was with Joanie and knew that they had to be together no matter what. Besides, as Meiki pointed out, it was easy enough to take a plane over to see him.

In New Hampshire they lived in Joanie's house, which had been the old fire station and had been converted into a home. It was on a large plot of land, with trees and outhouses, and was a lovely spot.

On Christmas Eve 1989, Meiki proposed very romantically and Joanie accepted at once. They were both incredibly happy and decided that the following May would be the perfect time to marry. Just as they were toasting their happiness with champagne, the phone rang. It was Joanie's twin brother, who wanted to wish them a happy Christmas and to share his exciting news: he had just proposed to his girlfriend and they were planning to marry in May. It was a delightful moment but Meiki and Joanie did not want to eclipse their news, so said nothing of their plans to anyone.

Joanie's brother Doug planned a big family wedding in Texas, so Meiki and Joanie felt there was no need to have another lavish do at the same time. They decided that they would get married a few days later in a quiet, low-key event at her parents' home. In fact, they kept it so quiet that they told me only a week beforehand, when Meiki rang to wish me a happy Mother's Day (in the USA, as in Germany, Mother's Day is the second Sunday in May).

After he had told me the news, I put the phone down, both delighted for them and desperate to be there myself. I told Ray and then rang Babette.

'Your brother is getting married next week — and not because Joanie's pregnant!' I said.

We decided that Babette and I would fly out, as it was such short notice that nobody else in the family could get there and, besides, Meiki had already said that he wanted something small and intimate. We arrived in time to attend Doug's wedding in Dallas, and I know one or two of the guests were wondering why Meiki's mother and sister were there. But, as the reception drew to a close, Joanie said a few words and then Meiki made the announcement that he and Joanie were getting married as well — and everyone understood. It made Doug's wedding an even happier occasion, as we all celebrated the two marriages.

The following day we drove to Georgetown in Texas, to Joanie's parents' home, a four-hour drive through beautiful, empty countryside, with fields and fields of brightly coloured flowers. We drove through a sandstorm too (our second experience of extreme weather, because while we were in Dallas we visited South Fork, the setting of the famous TV show *Dallas*, and watched a tornado sweep across it, putting out all the lights).

We stayed with Joanie's parents in their house just outside Georgetown and I was struck immediately by how the layout resembled the old brick factory house in the Wartegau. There were four wings, each with a double bedroom and bathroom, so that when any of their three children came home they had their own quarters. It was a beautiful place, and perfect for the intimate family occasion that Meiki and Joanie wanted.

Three days later a judge who was a friend of the family officiated at the quiet wedding ceremony. Babette and I spent hours wrapping white net round the balustrade on the veranda and hanging white crêpe-paper bells all around. When Meiki and Babette were babies, they each had little cuddly toy rabbits, which we called 'schubbers', short for *Schnupperhase*, which means 'sniffing hare'. Unknown to him I had taken his schubber out to America with me and I hung it among the decorations. Halfway through the ceremony he caught sight of it and his face lit up. I will never forget that wonderful day in May 1990.

Meiki and Joanie were very happy together. They both loved animals and their house was always full of them. Joanie had an elderly cat and Meiki took his cat with him. They acquired a spaniel, Ashley, who was always known as Crashley because of his habit of bumping into things, and more cats followed. Joanie shared Meiki's love for motorbikes, although nobody could ever match his passion for bikes, which he'd had since he was old enough to sit astride one. He loved tinkering with cars and bikes, and could take apart anything mechanical and put it back together again.

Meiki needed to find his feet and a new career. At first, he had lots of different jobs, working in a gun factory, as a painter and decorator, in a gym, as a gardener, in a garage, as a car salesman, to name but a few. He was also a volunteer fireman (appropriately enough, as he lived in an old fire station) and ambulanceman, as well as a trained paramedic, so he soon became well known and popular within the community.

He was also a talented cartoonist, and we all have hand-drawn cards he sent us at Christmas, birthdays and other special occasions.

Through his voluntary work as a fireman and an ambulanceman, Meiki got to know a lot of people.

A friend asked him if he would like to go to Police Academy and he said he really would. He had to get his American citizenship, but when that came through he started at the Academy, training to become an officer.

But then the idyll was shattered. We were all devasted when Meiki was diagnosed with testicular cancer.

Testicular cancer is curable, but Michael had ignored the symptoms. For example, he'd suffered from backache for a while, but he and Joanie had been helping to build an extension to the house, a triple garage with a floor on top, so he thought he had pulled a muscle doing the labouring, or even lifting a patient when he was called out as an ambulanceman.

I also remember how in the November of 1996, just months before the diagnosis, we visited him in America and I had been worried because after dinner, Meiki would be almost falling asleep, instead of chatting and playing cards, which we usually did. I said, 'Meiki, are you getting enough sleep? You're not pushing yourself too hard, are you?'

With the two volunteer services he was in, fire

and ambulance, he could be called by a bleeper at any time, day or night. He was very conscientious and would leap out of bed the minute it went off. 'No, Mum, I'm fine, really. Just a little tired.' He smiled at me, so I didn't go on at him. Other than that, he seemed very happy.

I wish now, with hindsight, that I had made him go to a doctor there and then. As it was, he didn't go until the following March, and by the time he was diagnosed the cancer had spread to his spine and lungs.

It was a terrible time of great grief and heart-break, but of hope too. We were all determined to help Meiki in every way and he had also resolved to fight it. He and Joanie had been married less than eight years and he wanted many more years of happiness with her. So they tried everything, open to any possible course of treatment. His medical bills were horrendous. Insurance covered the bulk of it, but we had to raise a lot more. Everybody joined in. One of Ray's firms in the building in Piccadilly had a special fund for hardship cases and they donated generously. Babette and I walked from Piccadilly to Hampton Court, sponsored by all our friends and family. It was twenty-three miles and despite the fact that I am registered disabled because of a back injury I suffered in 1988, I managed it. I spent the next five days in bed, totally kaput, but I didn't mind in the least: it felt right to share Meiki's pain just a little bit.

It is easy to look back and wish you had done things differently. If we had known he would not get better, we could have given him a superb fourteen months of life and pure pleasure, doing all the things he wanted to do. He would not have had to endure the gruelling months of treatment that reduced him to a shadow of himself. But we had to try: if we hadn't, we would always have regretted it. It meant that Meiki had to endure a very miserable time. The radiotherapy and chemotherapy meant that he could not keep down food, he was constantly sick, and always cold and shivering.

I travelled between America and home twelve times in the fourteen months Meiki was ill. It was very difficult, made harder by the fact that Ray had to have a triple heart bypass during this time and needed me back here as much as Meiki did out there, and I wanted desperately to be with both of them.

Meiki was being treated at the Hitchcock Medical Center in the town of Lebanon and there is a famous fish restaurant there, the Weather Vane, where we ate many times when he was well. Meiki loved the atmosphere, all scrubbed wooden tables and enormous platters of fish. One day, when he was very ill, we left the hospital after a chemotherapy session and he said to me and Joanie, 'Shall we go to the Weather Vane?'

We looked at each other in astonishment, because he hadn't eaten properly for months. He ordered a clam chowder, then a lobster, which came with a bib because the butter ran down his chin, and he even had a dessert, an iced fruit cup. The portions were, as ever, vast. We sat in the window and the sunlight streamed in on us, as if it were blessing us. He tucked into it all with relish and it was wonderful to see – it was a bigger meal than he would have tackled when he was well. Joanie and I watched in amazed pleasure, so engrossed in him eating that we could only pick at our own food.

Sadly, by the time we had driven home, three quarters of an hour away, he could not remember eating. He was fading fast and this was his one last good meal and, by some sort of alchemy, it did not make him sick.

Just a few weeks before he died he said to me, 'Mum, I don't want to be this ill any more.'

What could I reply to that? I could only put my arms round him and hold him close, longing with all my heart that I could make him well again. When your children are small, you can make things better for them with a sticking plaster and a cuddle. I felt so helpless. I would have done anything to change places with him. Meiki was only thirty-four and had so much to live for.

My deepest regret is that I wasn't there when he died. I couldn't get a flight and arrived a day too late. He died with Joanie and his best friend Steve Marshall, another police officer, at his side, and he knew I really loved him, because we never left anything unsaid.

How can anyone explain the grief for a dead child? It is unnatural to bury your own children. The death of a parent, a partner or a sibling is very sad, but we know that we have to face these things at some time. The death of her own child is something no mother expects or prepares for, even when she knows that child is dying.

I would give anything, anything in the world, for one last day with Meiki. I would walk through the battlefields, hear the anger of the guns, hide in the ditches, come face to face with the plunderers and the witch – anything, if I could see, hear and touch my beloved son just once more. The years have passed but time does nothing to lessen grief.

The Queen Mother said a very wise thing: 'Grief does not get any better, but you get better at dealing with it.'

I have gone through all the stages that, I know, others have experienced. There is nothing unique about my loss, except to me. I have cried, and still cry, every day at some memory, some thought that catches me unawares at the oddest of moments. My handsome, kind, generous, loving son, who would by now have been a wonderful police officer, has gone and I can never have him again. It is the cruellest, hardest blow ever inflicted on me by life.

Meiki's funeral was huge. The church had a big staircase, and it was lined with ambulancemen, firemen and policemen, all in uniform. Meiki, too, was in uniform, in his coffin. Opposite the church, up the hill, was the fire station, and it was all kitted out with trestle tables and benches, all laden with food and drink. We were presented with a rose and two flags, one the American flag and the other the flag of New Hampshire. I gave the American flag to Babette. There were reports of the funeral and glowing tributes to Meiki in all the local papers. Although he hadn't finished his police training course, Meiki was given his police badge and became an Officer Emeritus, the first ever in New Hampshire, before he died. It meant a great deal to him.

Steve Marshall, his best friend, delivered a moving eulogy and Steve's words explain Meiki as he was seen by other people. I, his mother, loved him, but when I heard Steve's speech I knew that my son had touched so many more lives and was loved by so many more people than I could guess.

Steve said that when he asked others for the words they would use to describe Mick, the four that came up all the time were 'friendly, compassionate, passionate and funny'. The two had first met when Meiki, in his role as a voluntary fireman, turned up to help Steve, who had been called to a dog that was entangled in cable. It was entirely appropriate that

us envious. They were always doing TV family things: little notes to each other; small, inexpensive but meaningful gifts; spur-of-the-moment trips and events. They always took the opportunity for a kiss, hand squeeze or hug and yes, even the dreaded baby-talk. Because that was the real Mick, and their moments together after his sickness were true and genuine, not a reaction to a tragic situation. Joan was his life, he was hers.

His passion for police work I am proud to say I got to see more than anyone else. He was so passionate about the profession and the people in it that he worked diligently to learn the best techniques from all the officers in the area.

His passion for life continued to the very end. As we would take our late-night patrols, we would talk as only partners can in a cruiser. We discussed life, we discussed death. Only once did he tell me that he didn't think he would survive the cancer. Only once did I see him cry. He did this away from Joan, to protect her, although she knew long before. His only fear in dying was that Joan would be alone, or more importantly he would be without her. But he was more afraid of living and becoming totally dependent on Joan, Mum, me and others. He knew that above all else he did not want many lives changed to prolong his. He was the one people called when they needed help or to be taken care of. It was difficult for him to be the one needing care.

Mick continued to show his passion for life all through the last hours of his life. As his condition started to deteriorate, he knew death would come. I knew his life was going to end, but when outside forces took control of him, and Joan and I were holding his hands, he looked me straight in the eye. It was a look that said 'I'm not going to go gracefully, I'm not going to roll over and let it take me'. He was telling Death: 'You want me, you fight me for it.' As consciousness left him he still refused to go. Joan kissed him, gave him her blessing to go. When the machines were switched off, he raised his head slightly, turned towards Joan, and Mick was finally in a place with no pain.

Mick was my partner and my best friend.

Michael

The day we first met, I remember it still.
You'd clog down a gear, slam your
   visor over your face,
The others in our gang would always
   give chase.

Pulling up in Andy's back yard every
   night, all weekend,
Always a problem to sort or a bike
   to mend,
Or just hanging around drinking coffee
   or tea,
A group of young friends, together and free,

Determined to be independent, money
   was sparse,
But enough for two bikes on the road,
   six more on the grass.
You just had to have them, you may need
   them for a part,
You couldn't let them go, you didn't have
   the heart.

When we went our separate ways it wasn't
   the end,

You were entwined in my life, still my
　　best friend,
You found new ventures, new scenes and
　　new mates,
But everything changed once you'd been to
　　the States.

It was hard not to be selfish, I didn't want
　　you to go,
You were my confidant, best friend, I would
　　miss you so,
But you were determined, you had found
　　something quite rare,
Something so special with Joan, you wanted
　　to be there.

And if God showed you no mercy by
　　taking your life,
We must be so grateful He gave you such a
　　wonderful wife,
You had found a happiness that most of us
　　never know,
In a beautiful country with someone who
　　loved you so.

But when you got sick you were so far
    away,
It was so very hard, we could only hope
    and pray,
That you knew we were thinking of you,
    every day,
And wishing we could be there to help in
    some way.

You still loved to ride, right up to the end,
To feel at one with the road, to hang on to
    each bend,
To pull out of the garage, put everything
    else aside,
Just you and your bike, to feel that rush,
    to ride.

You were so determined you would get well
again,
It wasn't an 'if' it was always a 'when',
You fought this thing with all of your might,
It was your character never to give up
    the fight.

I can find no answers to why you had to go,

Or how to cope, when we miss you so,
I've concluded we must keep you alive
   in our head,
And believe that you are somewhere
   better instead.

And believe that we'll meet again, in some
   place unknown,
Where we can all be together, no one
   left alone,
But still, I find it so hard to make sense
   of the reason why
We are all here today, to remember and to
   say goodbye

To someone so special, but who got so sick
You changed my life for ever, I'll never
   forget you:

                  I miss you, Mick.

A few weeks after the funeral we had a memorial service for Meiki in Esher, and Joanie and some of his colleagues, including Steve and Meiki's police chief Jim Benoit, came over for it. Last summer, we went back to the Weather Vane, where Meiki had

I have written a great deal about my son and not much about my daughter Babette. This is no reflection on my love for her, which is every bit as big as my love for Meiki. She is alive and lives near me, we talk every day and we share our lives in a way I no longer can with Meiki. I have no need to write my tribute to her: we are living it. She is a wonderful, caring daughter and an excellent mother.

Babette, who is known as Babs to all her friends, is married to Graham. He has three sons by his first marriage: Stuart, Charlie and Ryan. They see each other regularly and all live within half a mile. Babette and Graham have two children, AJ (Aaron Joseph) and Amy-Lou (Amy Louise Michelle). Babette never knew the full names of my father and mother, and yet she has included 'Joseph' and 'Louise' in her children's names, both names of my parents. AJ is a wonderful grandson. He is very much like Meiki and we are very proud of him. He plays football for Cobham and I love to go and cheer him and his team on. He likes to stay over with us and doing 'man' things with Ray, like playing snooker, pool, cards and games – or just talking things over.

Amy-Lou is much older than her seven years.

She loves to draw and write stories, something that started before she was five. We think she is an old soul and, if there is such a thing as reincarnation, Amy-Lou has definitely been here before. She often says the most incredible things for her young age. Once, when Ray was trying to suck up some crumbs with a hand-held 'dustbuster' and got a little frustrated because it wouldn't work properly, Amy said, 'Dadad, don't blame the tools if you can't or don't want to do the job.' She wasn't even five years old then.

Babette and Graham have very busy lives: she works in PR and Graham is a warehouse manager. They are very dear to us and I adore my grandchildren. We are also very close to Ray's four children and their wives and children.

Ray and I now live in a spacious flat in the centre of Esher, because we no longer wanted to have to maintain a garden. As well as having had a heart bypass, Ray is diabetic. I also have my health problems: I have had breast cancer and am still being treated for it, but after having an operation and a course of radiotherapy, I hope to make a full recovery and become a government success statistic by surviving for more than five years. More debilitating is the polymyalgia rheumatica (PMR) I suffer from, which cripples me and for which I have to take steroids. The steroids have caused plenty of other problems too. But life goes on and we can't change anything – we just have to make the best of what it throws at us.

———

Occasionally, when I am feeling sorry for myself, I wonder if Eva and I used up all our good luck in our walk across Germany, because neither of us had good health afterwards. But then I remember what my grandfather told me, that I had inherited his luck – and I know that he was right. Not only have I known great happiness but I have now been given the opportunity finally to put on paper the story of Eva's and my unbelievable journey, and to reflect on the enormous luck we had to come through it alive. Without that, there wouldn't have been anything else at all.

I hope that I've been able to share some of my luck by giving back to others who needed something – care, compassion or sometimes just a smile, a hug, a helping hand or a little time to listen.

'Life is what you make it!' Mutti used to teach us. And I believe that I have made mine as well as I could.

Of course there are misfortunes and unhappiness, as in any life. But usually I don't think about these. I don't want anyone to feel sorry for me. I have had a good and interesting life, and I am happy with it.

Today, my husband says I am more English than the English. I think and dream in English, and when I return to Germany it takes me a couple of hours to adjust to hearing my own language being spoken all around me. I still cook traditional German food and I serve my guests Stollen and poppy-seed cake and apfelstrudel (everyone's favourite), so I suppose I still make my home life a little bit German. But England is definitely home.

Yet the older I get, the closer I feel to my childhood. The body may age, but inside we remain the same people we always were, and the most lasting imprint on our lives and our personalities is made when we are children. My journey with my sister is always with me, deeply embedded in my thoughts and my memories. In thirty-three days, just a little over a month, I saw and experienced events that together were woven into a tapestry of horrors: I saw death and destruction, and I experienced terror, hunger and confusion. But if this is the warp, the weft is compassion, humour and great love, all of which played their part in our journey. Now, towards the end of my life and with so many experiences behind me, I can say with great certainty that love is the strongest thread in my life. The love my sister Eva gave me on that long walk, the way she battled to protect me at whatever cost to herself, lives with me on a daily basis and has, I hope, shaped all my dealings with others. Her love for me made all our terrible experiences bearable. I hope and pray that the love we all had for my son Michael made it easier for him to bear his illness and death.

For myself, I am sustained daily by my love for my husband Ray, for my daughter and her family, and for all the rest of our extended family and my many friends.

Love has been the theme of my life.

Epilogue

I have told you my story, but there are so many other people involved, especially members of my family, that I want to give you an update about what happened to them all.

My Parents

My father died in November 1966, after a series of strokes left him partially paralysed. Mutti eventually left the apartment she loved in old Horn and moved into a nursing home in Flottbek, just across the road from my sister Eva and her family. It was a beautiful place, a big house split into individual apartments, and hers was furnished with her own belongings. The home was run by an organisation associated with the Froebel Institute, where she had been educated, so it was full circle for her. Eventually, when she became too frail to stay in her own apartment, she moved into a wing where she received full-time nursing care. She died in 1990, at the age of eighty-six.

The evening before she died, the nursing sister came in to turn off the light and say goodnight, and Mutti said, 'I want to say a great big thank you to everyone who was wonderful to me.' She never woke up. It was a peaceful death, all any of us can ever wish for.

Eva

She and Kurt had two daughters, Angelika and Gunda. Eva's health was never good and she was very ill with asthma all her life, which left her debilitated. When her daughters were older, she ran a crèche for babies up to a year old at the large house she and Kurt lived in. Looking after the babies, whose mothers were students at the university, helped her health and there was even an article about her in the local newspaper, under the headline 'Very Ill Woman is Healed by Babies'. The crèche was beautifully organised and I used to love going there to cuddle the babies.

Until her death, we talked on the phone three times a week or more and visited each other regularly. Sometimes we would have what we called 'Sisters' Day', when we'd spend time together, just the two of us. Inevitably we'd reminisce about our long walk. We'd laugh, cry and remember our terror. One of us would say something like 'Can you still see the face of the witch?' and we'd be off, reliving those weeks. Most of all we'd talk about the incredible kindness we encountered from strangers, families who took us in and gave us shelter, and soldiers, whether they were American, British or German.

But our wartime memories didn't dominate everything; we talked all the time about other things too. There was an incredible bond between us. Eva and Kurt had a caravan, and we would go with them on trips to the seaside or the mountains, where the pure air helped her breathing.

Although Eva's health was poor, she always said,

'If only I can outlive Mutti.' She did, but only by four months, dying in January 1991, aged only sixty-five. Her lungs were weakened by asthma and she had pleurisy. In the months before she died she lost a lot of weight and even though she was hungry she could not hold down any food. Eva only developed asthma after Ruth died and, since Eva died, I myself have started to suffer from it. It is an odd coincidence – perhaps we sisters have handed it on to each other.

When Eva died I was distraught. I had lost both her and Mutti, my two angels, so close to each other. It was a very difficult time for me.

Kurt is still alive, living in a nursing home in Hamburg. Angelika has four children and lives in Hamburg. Gunda followed me and Henning into working for Lufthansa, but has now switched to Malaysian Airlines and lives south of Perth in Australia.

Uncle Willi and Aunt Hilda

Uncle Willi and Aunt Hilda divided their time between Hamburg, where their daughter Thekla lives, and the USA, where their sons Ulrich and

Volker made their homes. They spent six months of the year in each country. Uncle Willi died in 1959, aged only fifty-seven, and Aunt Hilda in 1989, aged eighty-six.

Thekla

Their oldest child married and has a daughter, Oliva. She is now a widow, and still lives in the house in the Jenfeld district of Hamburg that she and her parents built after the war on their land. She lives on the upper floor, and below live her daughter and son-in-law and their son. She spends a lot of time tending her beautiful garden.

Ulrich

He died in 2004, having moved to America soon after the war. Because his father, Uncle Willi, had been born in New York (more or less by chance: his mother was travelling when she broke a leg and had to stay there until after the birth) Willi always had dual nationality, which he passed to his children. Ulrich joined the US army and remained as madcap as he had been as a child. He believed in UFOs and thought he had been abducted by aliens.

He married twice and has two daughters from his first marriage. His first wife Thea is a really good friend of mine.

Volker

'My twin' lives in Florida and we are still very close: Ray and I often go out there to stay with him and his family. In Germany, when we were young, Volker did not think much of school but at the age of fourteen he went to live in the USA and there he graduated from high school. He discovered his skills as a businessman and has always been his own boss. He deals in cars, but they are rather specialised ones in the American market, all German and British models like Mercedes, BMW, VW, even Rolls-Royce and MG. He also sells boats, which is his real love, as he is happiest when he is out on his own boat, a beauty with a huge forty-foot mast. She was badly damaged in one of the hurricanes that hit Florida and swept two miles down the Indian river, but she is now back on the water. Volker has left his car business to be run by his wife Michelle, although he is still very involved, travelling to car auctions in

Orlando or Palm Beach, and driving across the States to deliver cars. He loves visiting boat shows, where he knows a great many people. He and Michelle have two sons, Hans and Brent, both great boys. With his first wife Maggie he has two children, Keith and Ellen, and Ellen has presented him with three grandchildren, Tristan, little Maggie and the baby Makena.

Whenever we are together we are still like brother and sister. Ray plays the piano and we sing together. His home is a beautiful house with stunning gardens and we feel very much at home there. Michelle is one of my best friends and when she learned that I was writing this book she arranged an 'English tea party' in her garden in my honour. I was very touched.

Aunt Irma and Uncle Hermann

Aunt Irma and Uncle Hermann bought an apartment in Hoheluft in Hamburg, where their son Henning still lives. Aunt Irma died in 1974 and Uncle Hermann in 1979.

Henning

We still refer to him as 'little Henning' and he followed me into working for Lufthansa. He had a really interesting job looking after the famous people who used the airline, so he has met lots of politicians, actors, actresses, film stars and musicians. He is retired now and he never married. His life is an incredible social whirl: if you ring Henning and catch him at home you feel you have really achieved something. There is not a play, a show, a concert or an exhibition in Hamburg that Henning has not been to, unless he missed them because he was travelling to Thailand, Australia or other exotic places.

Aunt Else

My father's sister, who lived near Berlin, and her family were in East Germany after the partition of the country between the Allies. Uncle Artur died soon after the war. One of her sons, Günther, never returned from the war. The other two are Horst, who is now dead, and Heinz, who is still alive. Her youngest child, Ruth, was the same age as me. She and her mother used to visit us in the

West, but the conditions laid down by the East German government meant that they were not allowed to take money out of the country, so my father always had to pay for their fares and all their spending money, and send them back with bags full of goodies. Although there was only three weeks' difference in our ages, when we met as teenagers Ruth always seemed much older than me. She and her mother were very dowdily dressed by our standards. Ruth married young, at eighteen or nineteen, a man twelve years older than her and has two children, now grown up of course. I remember her telling me that when her son was in school, he was pumped full of anti-West German propaganda and came home saying things like 'Adenauer is a schweinhund'. They did not dare contradict him in case he repeated what they said at school, which could have landed the whole family in trouble. Ruth and her husband still live at the same address they were at fifty years ago. I keep in touch by phone calls or letters on birthdays and at Christmas.

Ingo

My first boyfriend. He later married and has three sons and two daughters. I'm still in touch with his sister Heide, her husband Horst and daughter Maren.

Ilse

She lives south of Hamburg with her husband Eberhard. We are in regular contact and visit each other.

Ursi

My childhood friend, who used to make dresses with me and was with me in Geneva and later in London, sadly died in September 2000.

Miriam

She is coming to visit us this June.

The Sundermann Family

The kind people who lived near Posen have always kept in touch with my family. Mr and Mrs Sundermann are dead, and so is their son Fritz, who died in his twenties. But Heinz is still alive and I have visited him occasionally. He has two daughters and when they were little I remember they were fascinated by my blue eyeshadow, which was fashionable in England at the time but unusual in Germany. We spent a fun afternoon with me letting them try my make-up. Heinz worked for the railways until he retired.

Wandsbecker Chaussee

The apartment block has been rebuilt and there is still a bakery on the ground floor.

Hammer Park

Our little house was pulled down on 18 November 1955 and the park returned to its natural beauty. All trace of the British soldiers and the families who shared the park with them are gone. When I walked around it recently I tried to find the exact spot where our home stood, but even the fruit trees have gone and the lush grass bears no imprint of the shallow foundations. The allotments have also long gone, and the kindergarten building.

The park is, as it always was, the centre of the area's social life. There is a giant chessboard, with pieces the size of human beings; there is a hill called the *Liebesberg*, the love hill, because it seems to be the exclusive preserve of courting couples; there is a rose garden, a children's playground, a roller-skating area, tennis courts, the athletics track that was there in my youth, minigolf, and (how about this for a beautiful German word) a *Kleinkinderpinkelwinkel*. It means a 'little children's wee-wee corner' and is a small screened toilet area for little ones only.

The trees we climbed as youngsters remain: the park is justly proud of preserving some very old trees. There is a linden tree that is hundreds of years old and a very ancient oak that was damaged by a burning brand from a building during the bombing, but which is still standing.

Our house may not be there, but Hammer Park still feels like home.

Joanie

My son Meiki's wife has remarried, another Brit. She now lives across the road from the house that she and Meiki shared. We stay in close touch.

Ray's Four Sons

Stephen lives with his wife Patsy and their two sons James and Luke in Oxhey near Watford, Hertfordshire.

David now lives in Australia, near Perth, with his second wife Jane and two sons, Luke and Matthew. His first wife, Nicky, and their two children, Simon and Rachael, live in Bushey Heath, Hertfordshire.

Andrew and his wife Jo and their son Sam and daughter Jodie live in Bushey, Hertfordshire.

Matthew, the youngest, was at the time of writing this book on a world tour, spending some time in Australia with his brother David.

So, you see, with my two, AJ and Amy-Lou, and Graham's sons, we have thirteen grandchildren, and a lot of birthdays and school events to attend. They keep us busy and happy.

Acknowledgements

For many years I have been saying that one day I would write down the story of my childhood but somehow I have never found the time. Then my husband Ray heard an announcement on *Richard & Judy* on Channel 4; they were looking for the best true-life stories to publish. 'Now,' he said, 'you have no excuse. You have to write it.' So I did – and this is the result.

I have to thank Ray for the initial impetus, and for his patience and support during the months that I have been preoccupied with writing this book.

Acknowledgements

I must thank Richard Madeley and Judy Finnigan for coming up with such a brilliant idea, and for being so lovely to me when I made my first (very nervous) appearance on their programme. I must also thank the thousands of viewers who voted for my story to be one of those published, and I want to give a big thank you to Kate Elton, Emma Rose and everyone at Arrow Books for all their fantastic support and encouragement. I also want to thank Zoe Russell-Stretten, who made the mini-documentary about me and my sister Eva, which so captured the feeling of those times.

A very big thank you goes to Jean Ritchie, who is such a pleasure to work with. Jean, this is our book.

Most of all, I want to thank all the unnamed people, many of them soldiers, who helped us when we needed help so badly.

Finally, I give my thanks to my extended family and my many friends, for all the love I have enjoyed throughout my life.

Shattered

Mavis Marsh with Andrew Crofts

One terrible night in 1995, Mavis Marsh was woken to the devastating news that her son, Matthew, had been in an accident. Days later, doctors told Mavis and her husband Keith to give up all hope on their comatose son. The damage to his brain was too severe for him to recover. But Mavis and Keith refused to accept the diagnosis. For months they worked with Matthew, pleading with him to fight. Finally, almost half a year later, he suddenly started to respond . . .

Available August 2006

Betrayed

Lyndsey Harris with Andrew Crofts

From the age of six Sarah Harris was targeted by a vicious, manipulative but invisible enemy – and her life became a living hell. Before long she was suspended from school, alienated from her friends, completely bewildered and utterly terrified. Her happy childhood had been destroyed forever. For her mother, Lyndsey, it was a life beyond her worst nightmares. Suddenly, Lyndsey was fighting to keep her family together – and to save her daughter's sanity . . .

Available February 2007

arrow books